A HANDBOOK
TO
AGRA AND THE TAJ
SIKANDRA, FATEHPUR-SIKRI

A HANDBOOK
TO
AGRA AND THE TAJ
SIKANDRA, FATEHPUR-SIKRI

AND THE NEIGHBOURHOOD

E. B. HAVELL

WITH 14 ILLUSTRATIONS FROM PHOTOGRAPHS AND 4 PLANS

SECOND EDITION, REVISED, WITH APPENDIX

GYAN

Published by

GYAN

Gyan Publishing House
5, Ansari Road
Daryaganj, New Delhi-110002
Phone: 011-47034999, 9811692060
E-mail: books@gyanbooks.com

Distribution Network
gyanbooks.com
India, USA, Canada, UK, Australia, France

ISBN : 978-81-212-3469-6 (PB)
First Published, London, 1912

2nd Impression 2020

Printed at: Gyan Press, Delhi.

A Handbook to Agra and The Taj
Sikandra, Fatehpur-Sikri
Author: E. B. Havell

A HANDBOOK
TO
AGRA AND THE TAJ
SIKANDRA, FATEHPUR-SÎKRÎ
AND THE NEIGHBOURHOOD

BY
E. B. HAVELL
LATE PRINCIPAL, GOVERNMENT SCHOOL OF ART, CALCUTTA
AUTHOR OF "INDIAN SCULPTURE AND PAINTING," "THE IDEALS OF INDIAN ART,"
"BENARES: THE SACRED CITY," ETC.

WITH 14 ILLUSTRATIONS FROM PHOTOGRAPHS AND 4 PLANS

SECOND EDITION, REVISED, WITH APPENDIX

LONGMANS, GREEN, AND CO.
39 PATERNOSTER ROW, LONDON
NEW YORK, BOMBAY, AND CALCUTTA
1912

PREFACE

THIS little book is not intended for a history or archæological treatise, but to assist those who visit, or have visited, Agra, to an intelligent understanding of one of the greatest epochs of Indian Art. In the historical part of it, I have omitted unimportant names and dates, and only attempted to give such a sketch of the personality of the greatest of the Great Moguls, and of the times in which they lived, as is necessary for an appreciation of the wonderful monuments they left behind them. India is the only part of the British Empire where art is still a living reality, a portion of the people's spiritual possessions. We, in our ignorance and affectation of superiority, make efforts to improve it with Western ideas; but, so far, have only succeeded in doing it incalculable harm. It would be wiser if we would first attempt to understand it.

Among many works to which I owe valuable information, I should name especially Erskine's translation of Bâbar's "Memoirs;" Muhammad

Latif's "Agra, Historical and Descriptive;" and Edmund Smith's "Fatehpur-Sîkrî." My acknowledgments are due to Babu Abanindro Nath Tagore, Mr. A. Polwhele, Executive Engineer, Agra, and to Mr. J. H. Marshall, Director-General of the Archæological Survey of India, for kind assistance rendered. I am particularly indebted to Messrs. Johnston and Hoffman, of Calcutta, for allowing me to make use of their valuable collection of photographs for the illustrations.

In quoting from "Bernier's Travels," I have used Constable's translation, with Messrs. A. Constable & Co.'s kind permission. To the Editor of the *Nineteenth Century and After* I owe permission to make use of my article on "The Taj and its Designers," published in that Review, June, 1903.

CALCUTTA,
January, 1904.

PREFACE TO THE SECOND EDITION

SINCE the first edition of this book was published, several writers, including responsible historians like Mr. Vincent A. Smith, have attempted to revive the legend that the Taj was designed by an obscure Italian architect employed by Shah Jahân. Though no new facts or convincing arguments have been brought forward to strengthen the very flimsy foundation on which that legend rests, I have thought it desirable, besides making the necessary revisions for this new edition, to add an Appendix explaining once more in detail the grounds for rejecting it, which were first set forth in my article in the *Nineteenth Century and After.* The note on Hindu influence in Mogul architecture will, I hope, help to correct a very common misapprehension with regard to the history of Indian art and the evolution of Saracenic ar. in India.

E. B. H.

LONDON,
February, 1912.

CONTENTS

PAGE

HISTORICAL INTRODUCTION 3

The Great Moguls—I. Bâbar—Bâbar's Connection with Agra—II. Humâyûn—Interregnum: Shêr Shah—III. Akbar—Akbar's Connection with Agra—IV. Jahângîr—Jahângîr's Connection with Agra—V. Shah Jahân—The Monuments of Shah Jahân's Reign at Agra—VI. Aurangzîb—Agra and the Later Mogul Emperors—Agra in the Mutiny.

THE FORT 40

The Môtî Masjid—The Darshan Darwâza—The Dîwân-i-âm—Jahângîr's Cistern—The Tomb of Mr. Colvin—The Inner Mîna Bazar—The Chitor Gates—The Hindu Temple—The Machchî Bhawân—The Najîna Masjid—The Dîwân-i-Khâs—Jahângîr's Throne—The Baths—The Samman Burj—The Khâs Mahall—The Underground Chambers—The Angûrî Bâgh—Shîsh Mahall—The "Somnath" Gates—The Jahângîrî Mahall—The Salîmgarh.

THE JÂM'I MASJID 68

THE TAJ 71

The building of the Taj—The Intention of the Taj—Description.

ITMÂD-UD-DAULAH'S TOMB 86

THE CHÎNÎ-KÂ-RAUZA 92

THE RÂM BAGH 93

The Zuhara Bagh.

SIKANDRA 97

Akbar's Tomb—The Kanch Mahall—Sûraj-Bhan-kâ Bagh—Mariam Zâmâni's Tomb.

PAGE

OTHER BUILDINGS AND TOMBS AT OR NEAR AGRA . . 103

The Kâli Masjid—Alawal Bilawal—The Hammâm—The Roman Catholic Cemetery.

FATEHPUR SÎKRÎ 107

The Agra Gate—The Naubat Khâna—The Mint—The Daftar Khâna—The Palace—The Kwâbgâh—The Turkish Sultana's House—Hakîm's Baths—Pachîsî Board—The Dîwân-i-Khâs—The Ankh-Michaulî—The Yogi's Seat—The Hospital—The Dîwân-i-âm—The Panch Mahall—Miriam's Kôthî—Jodh Bai's Palace—Rajah Birbal's House, or Birbal's Daughter's House—The Hâthî Pôl and Adjoining Buildings—The Jâm'i Masjid, or Cathedral Mosque—The Buland Darwâza—The Stone-Cutters' Mosque—The Houses of Abûl Fazl and Faizi.

Bharatpur and Other Places in the Vicinity of Agra :—Bharatpur—Govardhan—Muttra—Bindrâban 133

APPENDIX I. THE DESIGNERS OF THE TAJ 137

APPENDIX II. HINDU INFLUENCE IN MOGUL ARCHITECTURE 142

INDEX 145

LIST OF ILLUSTRATIONS

TO FACE PAGE

THE TAJ MAHALL . . . . *Frontispiece*

PLATE I. A STATE DOCUMENT WITH SHAH JAHÂN'S "ROYAL HAND AND SEAL" 15

PLATE II. SHAH JAHÂN, FROM AN OLD INDIAN MINIATURE 29

PLATE III. THE INNER DELHI GATE, OR HÂTHÎ PÔL, AGRA FORT 40

PLATE IV. MARBLE BALCONY, OVERLOOKING THE INNER MÎNA BAZAR, AGRA FORT 52

PLATE V. THE SAMMAN BURJ, AGRA FORT 57

PLATE VI. INNER COURTYARD OF THE JAHÂNGÎRÎ MAHALL, AGRA FORT 66

PLATE VII. MARBLE SCREEN ENCLOSING THE TOMBS OF MUMTÂZ MAHALL AND SHAH JAHÂN 74

PLATE VIII. ITMÂD-UD-DAULAH'S TOMB, AGRA. . . . 87

PLATE IX. INTERIOR OF THE UPPER PAVILION, ITMÂD-UD-DAULAH'S TOMB 90

PLATE X. MARBLE SARCOPHAGUS ON THE UPPER STORY OF AKBAR'S TOMB, SIKANDRA 100

TO FACE PAGE

PLATE XI. INTERIOR OF THE DÎWÂN-I-KHÂS, FATEHPUR SÎKRÎ 112

PLATE XII. RAJAH BIRBAL'S DAUGHTER'S HOUSE, FATEHPUR SÎKRÎ 122

PLATE XIII. THE BULAND DARWÂZA, FATEHPUR SÎKRÎ 129

PLANS

AGRA FORT. PLAN OF THE PALACES 43

FATEHPUR SÎKRÎ. PLAN SHOWING THE POSITION OF THE BUILDINGS 107

FATEHPUR SÎKRÎ. PLAN SHOWING THE WALLS AND GATES 108

FATEHPUR SÎKRÎ. PLAN OF JODH BAI'S PALACE . . . 120

AGRA

AGRA

HISTORICAL INTRODUCTION

AGRA has two histories: one of the ancient city on the east, or left, bank of the river Jumna, going back so far as to be lost in the legends of Krishna and of the heroes of the Mahâbhârata; the other of the modern city, founded by Akbar in A.D. 1558, on the right bank of the river, and among Muhammadans still retaining its name of Akbarâbâd, which is intimately associated with the romance of the Great Moguls, and known throughout the world as the city of the Taj.

Of ancient Agra little now remains except a few traces of the foundations. It was a place of importance under various Hindu dynasties previous to the Muhammadan invasions of India, but its chequered fortunes down to the beginning of the sixteenth century are the usual tale of siege and capture by Hindu or Musalman, and possess little historical interest.

In A.D. 1505 Sultan Sikandar Lôdi, the last but

one of the Afghan dynasty at Delhi, rebuilt Agra and made it the seat of government. Sikandra, the burial-place of Akbar, is named after him, and there he built a garden-house which subsequently became the tomb of Mariam Zâmâni, one of Akbar's wives. The son of Sultan Sikandar, Ibrâhîm Lôdi, was defeated and slain by Bâbar at Pânîpat, near Delhi, in 1526, and from that time Agra became one of the principal cities of the Mogul Empire which Bâbar founded.

The Great Moguls.—I. Bâbar.

Though very few memorials of Bâbar's short but brilliant reign still exist at Agra, the life of this remarkable man is so important a part of the Mogul dynasty that it must not be passed over by the intelligent tourist or student of Mogul art. It was Bâbar's sunny disposition, and the love of nature characteristic of his race, that brought back into Indian art the note of joyousness which it had not known since the days of Buddhism. Bâbar is one of the most striking figures in Eastern history. He was descended from Tamerlane, or Tîmûr, on his father's side, and, on his mother's, from Chinghiz Khan. In the year 1494, at the age of twelve, he became king of Farghâna, a small kingdom of Central Asia, now known as Kôkân. His sovereignty, however, was of a very precarious tenure, for he was surrounded on all sides by a horde of rapacious, intriguing relatives, scrambling for the fragments of Tîmûr's empire. With hardly a trustworthy ally except a remarkably clever and courageous old grandmother, he struggled for three years to retain his birthright. Then, acting on a sudden inspiration, he made a dash for Samarkand, the ancient capital of Tîmûr, and won it. In his delightful memoirs Bâbar describes how, with boyish glee, he paced the ramparts himself, wandered from palace to palace, and revelled in the fruit-gardens of what was then one of the finest cities of Asia. But in less than a hundred days, most of his shifty Mongol troops, disappointed in not finding as much booty as they expected, deserted and joined a party of his enemies, who straightway attacked Andijân, the capital of Farghâna, where Bâbar had left his mother and grandmother. Before he could come to their rescue Andijân had fallen, and at the same time Samarkand, which he had left, was occupied by another of his numerous rivals. This double misfortune caused still more of his followers to leave him, and he found himself without a kingdom, except the little town of Khojend, and with only two hundred men. For almost the only time in his life he gave way utterly to despair. "I became a prey to melancholy and vexation; I was reduced to a sore distressed state and wept much."

Before long, however, Bâbar, rejoined by his mother and grandmother, whom the captors of Andijân had spared, taking advantage of another turn in the wheel of fortune, recovered his kingdom of Farghâna, but lost the greater part of it again through another desertion of his "Mongol rascals." A second time, with only a handful of men, he surprised and captured Samarkand (A.D. 1500). In the following year he rashly sallied out against Shaibâni, the most formidable of his adversaries, was defeated, and, after vainly trying to hold the city against the victors, was forced to fly under cover of the night. This time he did not weep, but consoled himself next morning by riding a headlong race with two of his companions. Reaching a village, where they found "nice fat flesh, bread of fine flour well baked, sweet melons, and excellent grapes in great abundance," Bâbar declared that in all his life he never enjoyed himself so much or felt so keenly the pleasures of peace and plenty.

He now took refuge among the hills near Uratipa, finding amusement in observing the life of the villagers, and especially in conversing with the mother of the headman, an old lady of a hundred and eleven, whose descendants, to the number of ninety-six, lived in the country round about. One of her relatives had served in the army with which Tîmûr had invaded India, and she entertained the future Emperor of Hindustan by telling him stories of his ancestor's adventures.

After several fruitless raids with the few troopers who remained faithful to him, he allied himself with his two uncles, Mahmûd and Ahmad Khân, in an attack against Tambal, one of the powerful nobles who had revolted against him and set up Jahângîr, his brother, on the throne of Farghâna. At a critical moment his uncles left Bâbar to the mercy of his enemy, and he was again forced to fly for his life, hotly pursued by Tambal's horsemen. He was overtaken by two of them, who, not daring to pit themselves against Bâbar's prodigious strength and courage, tried to inveigle him into a trap. Bâbar gives a moving description of this great crisis in his life. Thoroughly exhausted, and seeing no prospect of escape, he resigned himself to die :—

"There was a stream in the garden, and there I made my ablutions and recited a prayer of two bowings. Then surrendering myself to meditation, I was about to ask God for His compassion, when sleep closed my eyes. I saw (in my dream) Khwája Yakub, the son of Khwája Yahya, and grandson of his Eminence the Khwája 'Obaid-Allah (a famous saint of Samarkand), with a numerous escort, mounted on dappled grey horses, come before me and say, '*Do not be anxious, the Khwája has sent me to tell you that he will support you and seat you on the throne of sovereignty; whenever a difficulty occurs to you, remember to beg his help, and he will at once respond to your appeal, and victory and triumph shall straightway lean to your side.*' I awoke with easy heart, at the very moment when Yusuf the constable and his companions (Tambal's soldiers) were plotting some trick to seize and throttle me. Hearing them discussing it, I said to them, 'All you say is very well, but I shall be curious to see which of you dares to approach me.' As I spoke the tramp of a number of horses was heard outside the garden wall. Yusuf the constable exclaimed, 'If we had taken you and brought you to Tambal, our affairs would have prospered much thereby; as it is, he has sent a large troop to seize you; and the noise you hear is the tramp of horses on your track.' At this assertion my face fell, and I knew not what to devise.

"At this very moment the horsemen, who had not at first found the gate of the garden, made a breach in its crumbling wall, through which they entered. I saw they were Kutluk Muhammad Barlás and Babai Pargári, two of my most devoted followers, with ten or twenty other persons. When they came near to my person they threw themselves off their horses, and, bending the knee at a respectful distance, fell at my feet, and overwhelmed me with marks of their affection.

"Amazed at this apparition, I felt that God had just restored me to life. I called to them at once, 'Seize Yusuf the constable, and the wretched traitors who are with him, and bring them to me bound hand and foot.' Then, turning to my rescuers, I said, 'Whence come you? Who told you what was happening?' Kutluk Muhammad Barlás answered, 'After I found myself separated from you in the sudden flight from Akhsi, I reached Andiján at the very moment when the Khans themselves were making their entry. There I saw, in a dream, Khwája 'Obaid-Allah, who said, "*Pádishah Bâbar is at this instant in a village called Karmán; fly thither and bring him back with you, for the throne is his of right.*" Rejoicing at this dream, I rèlated it to the big Khan and little Khan . . . Three days have we been marching, and thanks be to God for bringing about this meeting."

[1] Bâbar's "Memoirs," translated by Erskine.

After this exciting adventure Bâbar rejoined his time-serving uncles, but was forced into exile again in 1503, when, at the battle of Akshi, the Khans were completely defeated by Shaibâni. Then he resolved to depart out of Farghâna and to give up the attempt to recover his kingdom. Characteristically, when foiled in one enterprise he entered upon another yet more ambitious. Joined by his two brothers, Jahângîr and Nâsir, and by a motley array of various wandering tribes, he swooped down upon Kabul and captured it.

The description of the new kingdom thus easily won, which fills many pages of the Memoirs, reveals another side of Bâbar's character—his intense love of nature. He gives minute accounts of the climate, physical characteristics, the fruits, flowers, birds, and beasts, as well as of the human inhabitants. In the intervals between his battles, or between his rollicking drinking parties, which for some years of his life degenerated into drunken orgies, we often find Bâbar lost in admiration of some beautiful landscape, or collecting flowers and planting fruit trees. Wherever he came Bâbar's first care was to dig wells and plant fruit and flower gardens. India owes much to the Great Mogul's love of horticulture.

When Bâbar had drilled his unruly Afghan subjects into something like order, he made, in

1506, one more unsuccessful attempt to crush Shaibâni. However, in 1510, when that doughty warrior was defeated and slain by Ismâ'îl, Shah of Persia, Samarkand fell once more into Bâbar's hands, as a vassal of the Shah. Eight months afterwards he was driven out again. From that time Bâbar gave up all hopes of re-establishing the empire of his ancestor Tîmûr, and turned his face towards India. In 1519 he gathered an army for his first expedition which was, however, more of a reconnaissance than a conquest. Four more attempts he made, until at last, in 1526, with only 10,000 men, he defeated the hosts of Ibrâhîm Lôdi, the last of the Afghan kings of Delhi, who, with 15,000 of his troops, were left dead on the field of Pânîpat.

Thus, after many struggles, Bâbar became "master and conqueror of the mighty empire of Hindustan," but he had to fight two more great battles before his sovereignty was undisputed—one in 1527 near Fatehpur Sîkrî, with the great chief of the Rajpûts, Rânâ Sanga of Chitor, and another in 1529 near Buxar, with the Afghans who had settled in Bengal. The next year Bâbar died in his garden palace at Agra. The nobility of his character was conspicuous in his death as it was in his life. He was devotedly attached to his eldest son, Humâyûn, who was seized with malarial fever while staying at his country estate at Sambhal. Bâbar had him removed by boat to Agra, but his physicians declared that the case was hopeless. Bâbar's own health had suffered much during his life in India, and he was terribly agitated by the news. When some one suggested that in such circumstances the Almighty sometimes deigned to accept the thing most valued by one friend in exchange for the life of another, Bâbar exclaimed that of all things his life was dearest to Humâyûn, as Humâyûn's was to him. He would sacrifice his own life to save his son. His courtiers entreated him to give up instead the great diamond taken at Agra, said to be the most valuable on earth. Bâbar declared that no stone could compare in value with his own life, and after solemnly walking round Humâyûn's couch, as in a religious sacrifice, he retired to devote himself to prayer. Soon afterwards he was heard to exclaim, "I have borne it away! I have borne it away!" Humâyûn began to recover, and, as he improved, Bâbar gradually sank. Commending his son to the protection of his friends, and imploring Humâyûn to be kind and forgiving to his brothers, the first of the "Great Moguls" of India passed away. He was buried at Kabul, in one of his beloved gardens, which, according to Tartar custom, he had chosen for his tomb, in "the sweetest spot of the neighbourhood."[1]

Bâbar's connection with Agra.

Bâbar's connection with Agra began immediately after the battle of Pânîpat. He sent forward Humâyûn, who occupied the town without opposition. The story of the great diamond referred to above is here recorded in the Memoirs. The Raja of Gwalior, slain at Pânîpat, had left his family and the heads of his clan at Agra. In gratitude to Humâyûn, who treated them magnanimously, and protected them from plunder, they presented to him a *peskesh*, or token of homage, consisting of a quantity of jewels and precious stones. Among these was one famous diamond which had been acquired by Sultan Alâ-ad-dîn. "It is so valuable that a judge of diamonds valued it at about half the daily expense of the whole world. It is about eight *mikkals*" (or about 280 carats). This is generally supposed to be the celebrated Koh-i-nûr.

Bâbar determined to establish the seat of his government at Agra, but was almost dissuaded by the desolate appearance of the country. "It

[1] For further particulars of Bâbar's history the reader is referred to the "Memoirs," or to Stanley Lane-Poole's admirable "Life of Babar," in the "Rulers of India Series" (Macmillan & Co.).

always appears to me," he says, "that one of the chief defects of Hindustan is the want of artificial watercourses. I had intended, wherever I might fix my residence, to construct water-wheels, to produce an artificial stream, and to lay out an elegant and regularly planned pleasure ground. Shortly after coming to Agra I passed the Jumna with this object in view, and examined the country to pitch upon a fit spot for a garden. The whole was so ugly and detestable that I repassed the river quite repulsed and disgusted. In consequence of the want of beauty and of the disagreeable aspect of the country, I gave up my intention of making a *charbagh* (garden house); but as no better situation presented itself near Agra, I was finally compelled to make the best of this same spot. . . . In every corner I planted suitable gardens, in every garden I sowed roses and narcissus regularly, and in beds corresponding to each other. We were annoyed by three things in Hindustan; one was its heat, another the strong winds, and the third its dust. Baths were the means of removing all three inconveniences."[1]

As I have mentioned above, there are very few vestiges remaining of Bâbar's city, of his fruit and flower gardens, palaces, baths, tanks, wells and

[1] See Appendix, Note II., on Hindu influence in Mogul architecture.

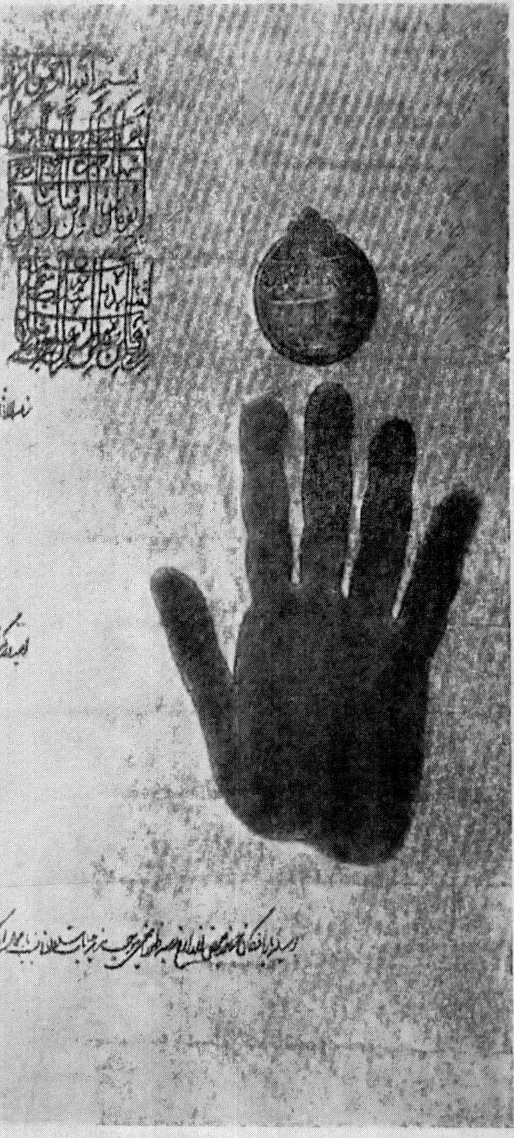

PLATE I.—A STATE DOCUMENT WITH SHAH JAHÂN'S "ROYAL HAND AND SEAL."

watercourses. The Râm Bagh (p. 93) is one of the gardens laid out either by himself or by one of his nobles, and the Zohra, or Zuhara Bagh, near it, contains the remains of a garden-house, which is said to have belonged to one of Bâbar's daughters. Opposite to the Taj there are traces of the foundations of the city he built. Bâbar planned, and his successors completed, the great road leading from Agra to Kabul through Lahore, parts of which still remain. Some of the old milestones can be seen on the road to Sikandra. Bâbar's account of the commencement of it is very characteristic: "On Thursday, the 4th of the latter Rebîa, I directed Çhikmâk Bey, by a writing under the royal hand and seal,[1] to measure the distance from Agra to Kabul; that at every nine *kos* he should raise a *minar*, or turret, twelve *gez* in height, on the top of which he was to construct a pavilion; that every ten *kos* he should erect a *yam*, or post-house, which they call a *dak-choki*, for six horses; that he should fix a certain allowance as a provision for the post-house keepers, couriers, and

[1] The State documents of the Mogul Emperors, "given under the royal hand and seal," were sometimes actually impressed by the royal hand. Plate I. reproduces part of a letter, addressed by Shah Jahan to an ancestor of the present Maharajah of Gidhour. In this letter the Raja Dalan Singh is informed that "the auspicious impress of the royal hand" is sent as a mark of royal favour, and he is commanded to proceed to Court to participate in the festivities and to pay homage to the Emperor.

grooms, and for feeding the horses; and orders were given that whenever a post-house for horses was built near a *khalseh*, or imperial demesne, they should be furnished from thence with the stated allowances; that if it were situated in a *pergunna*, the nobleman in charge should attend to the supply. The same day Chikmâk Padshahi left Agra."

The promptness of Bâbar's administrative methods is a striking contrast to the circumlocution of present-day departmentalism. There still exist remains of many splendid *sarais*, or halting-places, built along this road by different Mogul Emperors for their convenience, from the time of Bâbar down to Aurangzîb. One of the finest is the Nûrmahall Sarai, near Jalandhar, built by Jahângîr and named after his favourite wife. Edward Terry, who accompanied Sir Thomas Roe, James the First's ambassador at Jahângîr's Court, describes "the long walk of four hundred miles, shaded by great trees on both sides," and adds, "This is looked upon by the travellers who have found the comfort of that cool shade as one of the rarest and most beneficial works in the whole world."

II. Humâyûn.

Humâyûn, who succeeded Bâbar, had many of his father's amiable qualities, but none of his genius as a leader of men. He utterly failed in the attempt to consolidate the great empire which Bâbar had left him, and in 1539, or nine and a half years after his accession, he was completely defeated at Kanauj by Shêr Khan Sûr, an Afghan nobleman, who had submitted to Bâbar, but revolted against his son. Humâyûn found himself a fugitive with only a handful of men, and was eventually driven not only out of Hindustan, but even from the kingdom of Kabul. He then took refuge with the Shah of Persia. Shêr Khan Sûr, under the title of Shêr Shah, ruled at Agra until he died, five years afterwards. His son, Salîm Shah, or Sultân Islam, succeeded him, and reigned between seven and eight years, but on his death the usual quarrels between his relatives and generals gave Humâyûn, who in the meantime had got back Kabul with the aid of a Persian army, the opportunity to recover his position in Hindustan. This occurred in 1555, but Humâyûn's unfortunate reign terminated the same year through a fatal fall from a staircase in his palace at Delhi.

Humâyûn left no memorial of himself at Agra, but he is to be remembered for two circumstances: the first, that he was the father of the great Akbar, who succeeded him; and the second, that the plan of his tomb at Delhi, built by Akbar, was the model on which the plan of the Taj was based.

Interregnum: Shêr Shah.

Shêr Shah was the great builder, and a most capable ruler. In his short reign of five years he initiated many of the great administrative reforms which Akbar afterwards perfected. Fergusson, in his "History of Indian Architecture," mentions that in his time there was a fragment of a palace built by Shêr Shah in the Fort at Agra, "which was as exquisite a piece of decorative art as any of its class in India." This palace has since been destroyed to make room for a barrack, but probably the two-storied pavilion known as the Salîmgarh is the fragment to which Fergusson refers. The only other building of Shêr Shah's time now remaining in Agra is the half-buried mosque of Alawal Bilawal, or Shah Wilayat, in the *Nai-ki Mandi* quarter (see p. 102).

Shêr Shah's tomb at Sasseram, in Bihar, is one of the noblest monuments of the Pathân style, or the style of the earliest Muhammadan architects in India.

III. Akbar.

Akbar, "the Great," was born at Amarkôt, on the edge of the deserts of Marwar, about three years after the battle of Kanauj, when his father Humâyûn was a fugitive, driven from place to place by the adherents of Shêr Shah. At this time the treasury of the royal house was so reduced that, when Humâyûn indented on it for the customary presents to his faithful followers, the only thing procurable was a single pod of musk. With the cheerfulness which was the saving grace of Humâyûn, he broke up the pod, and distributed it, adding the pious wish, which seemed like prophetic insight, that his son's fame might fill the world like the fragrance of that perfume. Trained in the hard school of adversity, and inheriting the best qualities of his grandfather, Akbar was not long in restoring the faded fortunes of the Mogul dynasty. Like Bâbar, he succeeded to the throne at a very early age, and found himself surrounded by difficulties which would have overwhelmed a weaker character. Humâyûn had, indeed, fought his way back to Delhi and Agra, but he had by no means settled with all the numerous disputants for the sovereignty of Hindustan, which Sultan Islam's death had left in the field; and his departure from Kabul had been the signal for revolt in that quarter. Akbar, accompanied by Bairam Khan, the ablest of Humâyûn's generals, was in Sind when he received at the same time the news of his father's death and of the revolt of the Viceroy at Kabul. He was then little more than thirteen years old, but, like Bâbar under similar circumstances, he was prompt in decision and in action. Adopting Bairam's advice, which was contrary to that of all his other counsellors, he left Kabul out of account, and pushed on to Delhi against the forces of Hîmu, a Hindu general, and the most powerful of his foes, who had assumed the title of Raja Vikramâjit, with the hopes of restoring the old Hindu dynasty. On the historic plains of Pânîpat Akbar completely defeated Hîmu's army, and thus regained the empire which his grandfather had won on the same field thirty years before. This great battle was the most critical point in his career, and though Akbar had to undertake many other hard campaigns before he was absolute master of the empire, his position from that time was never seriously endangered.

Until his eighteenth year Akbar remained under the tutelage of Bairam, an able general, but unscrupulous and cruel. The high-minded, generous disposition of Akbar revolted against some of his guardian's methods, but he recognized that, for some years at least, Bairam's experience was necessary for him. In 1560, however, he took the administration entirely into his own hands. Bairam, in disgust, took up arms against his young master, but was soon defeated and taken prisoner. With his usual magnanimity, Akbar pardoned him, and sent him off to Mecca with a munificent present; but the revengeful knife of an Afghan put an end to the turbulent nobleman's life before he could leave India.

Akbar spent the rest of his long reign in elaborating the administrative reforms which have made him famous as the greatest ruler India has ever had. With the aid of able ministers, both Hindu and Muhammadan, he purified the administration of justice, keeping the supreme control in his own hands; enjoined absolute tolerance in religious matters; abolished oppressive taxes, and re-organized and improved the system of land revenue introduced by Shêr Shah. A minute account of Akbar's reign, of his policy, habits, and character, is given in the "Akbar-nâma," the history written by his devoted friend and Prime Minister, Abûl Fazl. No detail of state affairs was too small for Akbar's personal attention. Ability and integrity were the only passports to his favour, while bigotry and injustice were anathemas to him. Like Bâbar, he was fond of horticulture, and imported many kinds of fruit trees and flowers into India. Though he could neither read nor write, he had a great library of Hiṇdi, Persian, Arabic, Greek, and other books, and Abûl Fazl relates that every book was read through to him from beginning to end.

The most remarkable of all this remarkable man's

intellectual activities were his attempts to bring about a reconciliation of all the discordant religious elements of his empire. Badâyunî, one of his contemporary historians, but, unlike him, an orthodox Musalman, comments thus on Akbar's religious views: "From his earliest childhood to his manhood, and from his manhood to old age, his Majesty has passed through the most various phases, and through all sorts of religious practices and sectarian beliefs, and has collected everything which people can find in books, with a talent of selection peculiar to him and a spirit of inquiry opposed to every (Islamite) principle. Thus a faith based on some elementary principles traced itself on the mirror of his heart, and, as the result of all the influences which were brought to bear on his Majesty, there grew, gradually, as the outline on a stone, the conviction on his heart that there were sensible men in all religions, and abstemious thinkers and men endowed with miraculous powers among all nations. If some true knowledge were thus everywhere to be found, why should truth be confined to one religion, or to a creed like Islam, which was comparatively new, and scarcely a thousand years old; why should one sect assert what another denies, and why should one claim a preference without having superiority conferred upon itself?"

Near to his palace at Fatehpur Sîkrî he built an

Ibâdat Khâna, or Hall of Worship, for the discussion of philosophy and religion. There he received representatives of all religious sects, Muhammadans, Brahmans, Jains, Buddhists, Pârsîs, Jews, and Christians, and listened attentively to their arguments. He studied deeply religious books, and had the New Testament translated into Persian. He also invited Jesuit priests from Goa, and not only allowed them to build a church at Agra, but even attended a marriage service and interpreted the words of the sermon to the bride. Badâyunî says that "his Majesty firmly believed in the truth of the Christian religion, and wishing to spread the doctrines of Jesus, ordered Prince Murad (his son) to take a few lessons in Christianity by way of auspiciousness." The Jesuits, however, did not succeed in making Akbar a convert, for when his religious convictions were at last settled, he proclaimed as the state religion a kind of eclectic pantheism called Dîn-i-ilâhi, or "Divine Faith," with himself as the chief interpreter. Dispensing with all forms of priesthood, he simply recognized One God, the Maker of the Universe, and himself as God's vicegerent on earth. He rejected the doctrine of the Resurrection, and accepted that of the transmigration of souls. The Islamite prayers were abolished, and others of a more general character were substituted for them.

The ceremonial was largely borrowed from the Hindus.

The "Divine Faith" had no hold on the people, and its influence ceased with the death of its founder. It is even said that Akbar, on his death-bed, acknowledged the orthodox Muhammadan creed, but the evidence on this point is unreliable. Akbar's religious system had an important political bearing, for the keynote of his whole policy was the endeavour to unite with a bond of common interest all the diverse social, religious, and racial elements of his empire. He overlooked nothing which might further the object he had in view. He chose his ministers and generals indiscriminately from all his subjects, without distinction of race or religion. He allied himself in marriage with the royal Hindu families of Rajputâna. He sat daily on the judgment seat to dispense justice to all who chose to appeal to him, and, like the famous Hârûn-al-Rashîd, he would at times put on disguises and wander unattended among the people, to keep himself informed of their real condition and to check the malpractices of his officials.

Though Akbar unavoidably had bitter enemies among the more bigoted of his Muhammadan subjects, his wise tolerance of all beliefs and the generosity of his policy for the most part disarmed hostility from all sides. Certainly no ruler of India before or since succeeded so far in carrying out his object. He is still one of the great popular heroes of Hindustan; his mighty deeds in war and in the chase, his wise and witty sayings, the splendour of his court, his magnanimity and his justice, still live in song and in story.

Akbar died in the fort at Agra on October 13, 1605, in the fifty-first year of his reign, aged 63. He was buried at Sikandra, in the mausoleum commenced by himself, and finished by his son and successor, Jahângîr.

Akbar's connection with Agra.

The modern city of Agra, as stated previously, was founded by Akbar in 1558, opposite to the old city on the left bank of the river. He built the Fort, on the site of an old Pathân castle, and part of the palace within it. Agra was the seat of government during the greater part of his reign. He also built the great mosque and the magnificent palaces and public buildings of Fatehpur Sîkrî, which are among the most famous of the antiquities of India.

IV. Jahângîr.

The eldest surviving son of Akbar, Prince Salîm, on his accession to the throne in 1605, assumed the title of Nûr-ud-dîn Jahângîr (Light of the Faith, Conqueror of the World).

He was passionate, cruel, and a drunkard, but not without ability and force of character. As Prince Salîm he had instigated the assassination of the Prime Minister, Abûl Fazl, and probably hastened his own father's death by his violent conduct. There was, however, a reconciliation at the end, and Jahângîr endeavoured to atone for his behaviour by lavish expenditure on Akbar's tomb at Sikandra. He has also left many pious tributes to his father's memory in his autobiography. Jahângîr's favourite wife was the celebrated Nûr Mahall, who for twenty years was almost the supreme power in the imperial court. Her beauty attracted his attention while he was still Prince Salîm, but Akbar, disapproving of her as a daughter-in-law, gave her in marriage to Shêr Afsân, "the lion killer," a nobleman of Burdwân. After his accession, having treacherously procured the death of her husband, Jahângîr had Nûr Mahall removed to Agra and placed under the care of his mother. For many years she repulsed all Jahângîr's overtures, but when at last she consented to be his queen she became his most devoted wife. She accompanied him on all his travels, and Jahângîr consulted her in all important affairs of state. Sir Thomas Roe, James the First's ambassador, describes Jahângîr at Agra, taking his wife for an evening drive in a bullock cart, "the King himself being her carter." He affectionately changed her name from Nûr Mahall, "Light of the Palace," to Nûr Jahân, "Light of the World." The imperial coinage bore her name, and an inscription, "Gold has acquired a new value since it bore the name of Nûr Jahân." She even succeeded to some extent in controlling Jahângîr's drunken habits. She was a great patroness of the arts, and it is said that the Samman Burj, her apartments in the Agra palace, were decorated after her designs. Her charity was boundless; she was the especial protectress of orphan girls, and provided marriage portions for no less than five hundred from her private purse.

Nûr Mahall's father, Itmâd-ud-daulah, became Lord High Treasurer, and afterwards Wazîr, or Prime Minister. On his death his daughter built for him the magnificent tomb at Agra known by his name.

During Jahângîr's reign many Europeans—travellers, adventurers and others—flocked to the Mogul court. They were allowed free access to the palace, and Jahângîr frequently admitted them to join in his midnight carouses. He showed great favour to the Jesuit priests, and even allowed two of his nephews to be instructed in the Christian religion.

The violent temper of Jahângîr was inherited by his son, Prince Khurram, afterwards Shah Jahân, and the peace of his reign was frequently disturbed by open rebellion on the part of the Prince. In 1623 Shah Jahân actually sacked Agra, and his soldiers committed fearful atrocities on the inhabitants. He failed, however, to capture the fort, which contained the imperial treasury, and Jahângîr, no doubt remembering his own father's leniency towards himself, forgave his unruly son.

Jahângîr died in 1627, and was buried at Shâhdara, near Lahore, in a magnificent tomb prepared by Nûr Mahall. She herself retired to Lahore, and, though she lived till 1648, ceased to take any part in state affairs after his death. She was buried by her husband's side at Shâhdara.

Jahângîr's connection with Agra.

Jahângîr, for a great part of his reign, held his court at Lahore, or at Kabul. The chief monuments of his reign at or near Agra are Akbar's tomb at Sikandra (p. 97), and Itmâd-ud-daulah's tomb (p. 86), already mentioned. Part of the Agra palace, the Jahângîrî Mahall (p. 63), is named after him, though it is most probable that it was really built in Akbar's reign.

There are a few minor buildings of Jahângîr's

PLATE II.—SHAH JAHÂN, FROM AN OLD INDIAN MINIATURE.

time in Agra, such as the baths of Ali Verdi Khan in Chipitollah Street, the mosque of Motamid Khan in the Kashmîrî Bazar, and the tower known after the name of Buland Khan, the chief eunuch of Jahângîr's palace. These are of purely archæological interest.

V. Shah Jahân.

Shah Jahân, on his father's death, though only fourth in right of succession to the throne, speedily disposed of his brothers by means very commonly adopted in the Mogul royal families, and was enthroned at Agra in 1628. Soon afterwards he wreaked his vengeance on the Portuguese, who had taken part against him in his rebellion against Jahângîr, by destroying their settlement at Hûghli. A year after this, or in 1631, while on an expedition to suppress disorder in the Deccan, he lost his favourite wife, Mumtâz Mahall, the Lady of the Taj. For a long time the Emperor abandoned himself entirely to grief, and he remained faithful to her memory until his death.

The actual building of the Taj commenced in 1632. From this date until 1658, when Aurangzîb usurped the throne, was the most magnificent period of the Mogul Dynasty. The whole empire enjoyed comparative peace and prosperity. Shah Jahân's just and liberal government continued his father's and grandfather's policy of tolerance towards the Hindus, and his administration, though conducted with great pomp and splendour, did not press hardly upon the people. It was one of the greatest epochs of Indian architecture. Besides the Taj Mahall, the buildings erected during these years include four of the masterpieces of the Mogul period —the Jâm'i Masjid of Delhi, the Môtî Masjid, or Pearl Mosque, of Agra, part of the Agra Palace, and the great palace of Delhi, of which only a small portion now exists.

It is said that, as Shah Jahân advanced towards old age, he abandoned himself more and more to a life of pleasure and self-indulgence; but his last years were darkened by the same kind of family intrigues through which he himself had gained the throne. In 1657 the serious illness of the Emperor brought these intrigues to a head. His eldest son by Mumtâz Mahall, called Dârâ Shukoh, a gracious and generous prince, but headstrong and intolerant of advice, was appointed Regent. On receiving this intelligence, his younger brothers, Shuja, Viceroy of Bengal, and Murad, Viceroy of Gujerat, declared their independence, and marched upon Agra. Aurangẓib, the third son, a religious bigot, but the ablest and most virile of the brothers, hastened to join them, and, being placed in chief command, attacked Dârâ's army close to Agra, and completely defeated him. Three days afterwards he entered the city. Shah Jahân sent his chamberlain to order him to leave the city at once and return to his post in the Deccan, but Aurangzîb, affecting to believe that his father was dead, disregarded the order. He succeeded by bribes and promises in bringing over some of the principal nobles to his side, and being well informed by Rushanârâ, his younger sister, who was his equal in cunning and artifice, of all that went on in the palace, he baffled Shah Jahân's attempts to lay hands on him. At last, under pretence of arranging an amicable meeting with his son Mahmûd, Aurangzîb beguiled Shah Jahân into withdrawing his troops from the fort. Mahmûd immediately forced his way in with a picked body of men and seized the person of the Emperor. The plan succeeded so well that no attempt at a rescue was made.

The French traveller, Tavernier, who has left a complete record of the time, writes of this event: " It is most surprising that not one of the servants of the grand king offered to assist him; that all his subjects abandoned him, and that they turned their eyes to the rising sun, recognizing no one as king but Aurangzîb. Shah Jahân, though still living, passed from their memories. If, perchance, there were any who felt touched by his misfortunes, fear made them silent, and made them basely abandon a king who had governed them like a father, and with a mildness which is not common with sovereigns. For though he was severe enough to the nobles when they failed to perform their duties, he arranged all things for the comfort of the people, by whom he was much beloved, but who gave no signs of it at this crisis."

Shah Jahân remained confined in a set of apartments of the Agra Palace for seven years. He died in 1666, and was buried by the side of Mumtâz Mahall in the Taj. His captivity was shared by his favourite daughter, Jahânârâ, who, since the death of her mother, had ruled the imperial household and taken a prominent part in state affairs. She had actively supported the cause of Dârâ, and thus incurred the resentment of Aurangzîb. On her father's death she retired to Delhi, and lived there until 1681. Her simple grave, covered with grass, is in a quiet corner of the courtyard of Nizâmudîn's tomb, near Delhi, where the memory of her filial piety adds to the poetic charm of all the surroundings.

The Monuments of Shah Jahân's Reign at Agra.

The Taj Mahall (p. 72); the Jâm'i Masjid (p. 69); and the following buildings in the Fort: The Môtî Masjid (p. 43); the Dîwân-i-âm (p. 46); the Dîwân-i-khâs (p. 55); the Khâs Mahall (p. 59).

VI. Aurangzîb.

Agra is only concerned with the first seven years of Aurangzîb's reign, for, after the death of Shah Jahân, the court was removed to Delhi, and Agra was left with only a provincial governor to maintain its former magnificence. The unhappy Dârâ, after his defeat by Aurangzîb, made fruitless attempts to retrieve his fortunes, but was at last betrayed into the hands of his brother, who immediately put him to death. Aurangzîb lost no time in disposing of his other two brothers, and thus placed his succession to the throne beyond dispute.

The Princess Rushanârâ, as a reward for her treachery, was raised to the position formerly enjoyed by her sister Jahânara. The French physician Bernier, who resided twelve years at the Mogul court in the time of Aurangzîb, has left many minute and graphic records of the times. Here is a picture of Rushanârâ when she accompanied Aurangzîb on the march from Delhi to Kashmir :—

"Stretch imagination to its utmost limits, and you can conceive no exhibition more grand and imposing than when Rauchenara-Begum, mounted on a stupendous Pegu elephant and seated in a *mikdember*, blazing with gold and azure, is followed by five or six other elephants with *mikdembers* nearly as resplendent as her own, and filled with ladies attached to her household. Close to the Princess are the chief eunuchs, richly adorned and finely mounted, each with a wand of office in his hand; and surrounding her elephant a troop of female servants, *Tartars* and *Kachmerys*, fantastically attired and riding handsome pad-horses. Besides these attendants are several eunuchs on horseback, accompanied by a multitude of *pagys*, or lackeys, on foot, with large canes, who advance a great way before the Princess, both to the right and left, for the purpose of clearing the road and driving before them every intruder. Immediately behind Rauchenara-Begum's retinue appears a principal lady of the court, mounted and attended in much the same manner as the Princess. This lady is followed by a third, she by a fourth, and so on, until fifteen or sixteen females of quality pass with a grandeur of appearance, equipage, and retinue more or less proportionate to their rank, pay, and office. There is something very impressive of state and royalty in the march of these sixty or more elephants; in their solemn and, as it were, measured steps, in the splendour of the *mikdembers*, and the brilliant and innumerable followers in attendance; and, if I had not regarded this display of magnificence with a sort of philosophical indifference, I should have been apt to be carried away by such flights of imagination as inspire most of the Indian poets when they represent the elephants as conveying so many goddesses concealed from the vulgar gaze."[1]

Dramatic justice overtook the scheming Princess at last. In 1664 Aurangzîb fell dangerously ill, and, while he was unconscious, Rushanârâ, believing him to be dying, abstracted the signet ring from his finger and issued letters, as under the royal zeal, to the various Viceroys and Governors, setting aside the succession of the Emperor's eldest son by a Rajput Princess in favour of another son, a boy of six, by a Muhammadan sultana. She hoped by this means to keep the supreme power in her own hands during the long minority of the new Emperor. Aurangzîb unexpectedly rècovered, and became suspicious of his dangerous sister. The host of enemies she had created at court were not slow in taking advantage of the situation, and Rushanârâ soon afterwards disappeared—removed, it is said, by poison.

Aurangzîb ruled with a firm hand, and in strict justice according to the law of Islam, but though a man of great intellectual powers, of

[1] Bernier's "Travels"—Constable's translation.

marvellous energy and indomitable courage, he was wanting in imagination, sympathy, and foresight, the highest qualities of a really great ruler. He checked the dissolute conduct of the nobles, and set an example of industry and devotion to duty; but his narrow, bigoted disposition inclined him to distrust even his own ministers, so that, unlike his three predecessors, he was badly served by the lieutenants in whose hands the administration of the provinces rested. He surrounded himself with religious bigots of the Sunni sect of Muhammadans, who aided him in bitter persecution of the Hindus. Hardly anything of artistic or architectural interest was created under his patronage. Most of the great artists who attended Shah Jahân's court were dismissed as unorthodox or heretics, and many noble monuments were mutilated by the Emperor's fanatical followers on the ground that they contravened the precept of the Koran which forbids the representation of animate nature in art.

He died in 1707, eighty-nine years of age. The Mogul empire, surrounded by hordes of the enemies his bigotry and intolerance had created, was already tottering to its fall, and the star of the British raj was rising. Seventeen years before his death he had granted to Job Charnock a piece of land at Sutanati, the site on which Calcutta, so long the capital of our Indian empire, was to be built.

Agra and the Later Mogul Emperors.

Agra played a very small part in the history of the weak-minded and dissolute successors of Aurangzîb. Firokhshiyar, who reigned from 1713 to 1719, resided occasionally there. After his death disputes between various claimants to the throne led to Agra Fort being besieged and captured by Husein Ali Khân, a partisan of one of them, who looted the treasury of all the valuables deposited there during three centuries. "There were the effects of Nûr Jahân Begum and Mumtâz Mahal, amounting in value, according to various reports, to two or three crores of rupees. There was in particular the sheet of pearls which Shah Jahân had caused to be made for the tomb of Mumtâz Mahal, of the value of several lakhs of rupees, which was spread over it on the anniversary and on Friday nights. There was the ewer of Nûr Jahân and her cushion of woven gold and rich pearls, with a border of valuable garnets and emeralds." (Elliott.)

In 1739 Nâdir Shah of Persia, sacked Delhi, carried off Shah Jahân's famous peacock throne, and laid Agra also under contribution. The

Mahrattas next appeared on the scene. In 1764 the Jâts of Bharatpur, under Sûraj Mall, captured Agra, looted the Taj, and played havoc with the palaces in the Fort. They were joined by Walter Reinhardt, an adventurer, half French and half German, who sold his services for any work of infamy, and had only recently assisted in the murder of the British Resident and other Europeans at Patna. He afterwards entered the Mogul service, and was rewarded by a grant of a tract of country near Meerut, which remained in the possession of his family until recent times. He died at Agra in 1778, and was buried in the Catholic cemetery.

For the next thirty-nine years Agra was occupied by Mahrattas and by Mogul imperialists in turn. John Hessing, a Dutch officer in the employ of the Mahrattas, was Governor of Agra, in 1794, and died there in 1802. The next year it was captured by the British under General, afterwards Lord, Lake, and from that time until 1857 its history was uneventful.

Agra in the Mutiny.

Agra did not take any prominent part in the events of the Mutiny. A mob plundered the city, burnt the public offices, and killed a number of

Europeans; but the rioters left soon to join their comrades at Delhi. There was a small engagement outside the city. The British troops and the whole of the European population were afterwards shut up in the Fort until the capture of Delhi. The Lieutenant-Governor, Mr. John Russell Colvin, died there, and was buried in front of the Dîwân-i-âm.

THE FORT

The present Fort was commenced by Akbar in 1566, on the site of an older one constructed by Salîm Shah Sûr, the son of Shêr Shah. Its vast walls (seventy feet in height, and a mile and a half in circuit), its turrets, and noble gateways present from the outside a most imposing appearance. It contains within its walls that most exquisite of mosques, the Môtî Masjid, and the palaces of Akbar and Shah Jahân. The principal or north entrance is the Delhi Gate, nearly opposite to the railway station and the Jâm'i Masjid. Formerly there was a walled enclosure in front of this gate, called the Tripulia, or Three Gates, which was used as a market. This was cleared away by the military authorities in 1875. Crossing the drawbridge over the moat which surrounds the Fort, the visitor passes the outer gate, and by a paved incline reaches the Hâthî Pôl, or Elephant Gate (Plate III.), so called from the two stone elephants, with riders, which formerly stood outside the gate, on the highest of the platforms

Johnston and Hoffman, Photo.]

PLATE III.—THE INNER DELHI GATE, OR HÂTHÎ PÔL, AGRA FORT.

on either side of it. The statues and elephants were thrown down by order of Aurangzîb. There are four hollow placés in each platform, where the legs of the elephants were morticed into it.[1]

[1] These elephant statues have been a vexed point with archæologists. Bernier, in his description of Delhi, refers to two great elephants of stone, with their riders, outside of the Fort Gates. The riders, he says, were portraits of the famous Rajput chiefs Jaymal and Patta, slain by Akbar at the siege of Chitor. "Their enemies, in admiration of the devotion of the two heroes put up these statues to their memory." Now, Bernier does not say that the statues were put up by Akbar, but General Cunningham, inferring that Bernier meant this, propounded a theory that they were originally in front of the Agra Fort, which Akbar built, and removed to Delhi by Shah Jahân, when he built his new palace there. Keene, who discusses the question at length in his "Handbook to Delhi," accepts this suggestion. Neither of these authorities seems to have been aware of the existence of the marks of the feet on the platform in front of the Agra Hâthî Pôl. I have compared the measurements of these marks with the dimensions of the elephant which still exists at Delhi, and find that they do not correspond in any way. The Delhi elephant is a much larger animal, and would not fit into the platform at the Agra gate. General Cunningham's theory, therefore, falls to the ground. It is just possible that the Delhi elephants were intended to be copies of those placed by Akbar at Agra. Shah Jahân is not likely to have intentionally perpetuated the memory of the Rajput chiefs, but popular tradition or imagination may have fastened the story told by Bernier on to the Delhi statues. Elephants were so commonly placed in front of Indian palaces and fortresses that, except for this story, there would be no need to suppose any connection between those at Agra and those at Delhi.

Purchas, quoting William Finch who visited Agra in Jahângîr's time, describes the elephants at the Hâthî Pôl, but gives a different origin to the statues. "Beyond these two gates you pass a second gate, over which are two Rajaws in stone. It is said that they were two brother Rajputs, tutors to a prince, their nephew, whom the King demanded of them. They refused, and were committed ;

The gate is a fine example of the early Mogul style; it contains the *Naubat khâna,* or music gallery, where the royal kettledrums announced the Emperor's arrival or departure, and all state functions. It was also a guard-house, and probably the quarters of a high military officer, but it is certainly not, as the guides have it, the "Darshan Darwâza," or "Gate of Sights," described by William Finch, where the Emperor Jahângîr showed himself at sunrise to his nobles and to the multitude assembled in the plain below. The Darshan Darwâza was undoubtedly near the old disused watergate, which was joined to the royal apartments of the palace by a private passage, and answers to Finch's description of "leading into a fair court extending along the river." The Elephant Gate is at a considerable distance from the palace, and was never connected with it, except by the public road.

It is worth while to climb the top of the gate by the staircase on the right, inside the Fort. There is a fine view of the Fort, and beyond the walls the ever-beautiful white domes of the Taj appear in the distance. The Itmâd-ud-daulah is

but drew on the officers, slew twelve, and at last, by multitudes oppressing, were themselves slain, and here have elephants of stone and themselves figured." The expression "over" (the gate) has the meaning of "high up," and not, as Keene supposes, its more modern sense of "on the top of."

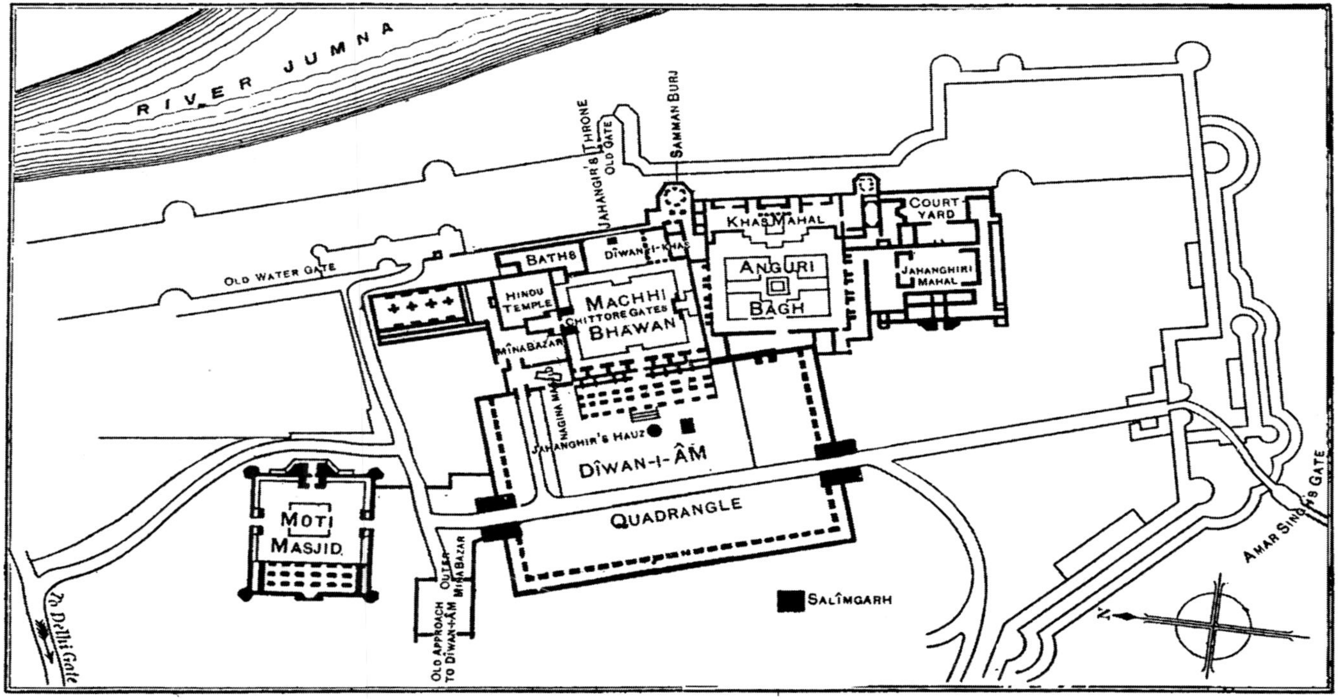

AGRA FORT—PLAN OF THE PALACES.

visible on the left. Towards the town you look down into the quadrangle of the Jâm'i Masjid. The pavilions on the súmmit of the great octagonal towers flanking the gate are finely carved, and bear traces of painting and enamelled tilework. Descending the staircase to the floors beneath, one can wander through the curious small chambers and look out from the balconies on the front of the gate.

The Môtî Masjid.

The road to the left after passing the Elephant Gate leads up to the entrance of the Môtî Masjid, or "Pearl Mosque," placed on the highest point of the Fort enclosure.[1] You pass on the left a building known as Dansa Jât's house, said to have been occupied by the Rajahs of Bharatpur when the Jâts held the Fort. It has been made hideous by modern additions which have converted it into officers' quarters.

The entrance to the Môtî Masjid is very plain and unpretending, so that one is hardly prepared for the beauty, purity, and the unaffected expression of an exalted religious feeling which characterize the interior. It is rare to find an Indian building in which the effect is produced

[1] The old Mogul road led directly from the Elephant Gate to the entrance of the Dîwân-i-âm. I understand that this road will be restored shortly by the Archæological Department.

with hardly any ornament, but solely by the perfection of proportions, beauty of material, and harmony of constructive design. The courtyard, in front of the mosque, with its arcades and gateways, is a noble setting to the Pearl, as the mosque is appropriately called. There is a subtle rhythm in the placing of the three domes over the seven arches of the mosque, which saves the whole design from monotony, while the marvellous grace of the contours, which is so characteristic of the finest of Shah Jahân's buildings, makes each dome grow up from the roof like a flower-bud on the point of unfolding. The octagonal pavilions at the four corners of the mosque, and the dainty little kiosques placed as decoration over the arches and over the gateways of the courtyard, echo the harmonies of the larger constructive details, and give completeness to the composition.

The interior of the mosque owes its dignity to the same greatness of style and perfection of the proportions. The three aisles are formed by massive piers of single blocks of marble. With all its simplicity, there is consummate art both in the placing of the ornament and in the beautiful springing of the arches from the supporting piers. The fine workmanship is worthy of the art.

On either side of the mosque there is a small chamber for the ladies of the zanana, with a window filled with a carved marble *grille* looking on to the interior. They could thus attend to the services of the mosque without being seen. The staircases on the right and left of the courtyard give private access to the apartments of the palace.

The Persian inscription inlaid in black marble under the wide, projecting cornice of the mosque is a poetic tribute to the beauty of the building and a panegyric of its founder. From it we learn that it was built by Shah Jahân, it took seven years to build, and cost three lakhs of rupees.

The dimensions of the courtyard, given by Fergusson, are 154 feet by 158 feet; and of the Mosque: length, 159 feet; depth, 56 feet, internally.

The Dârshan Darwâza.

Nearly opposite to the Môtî Masjid, you pass on the left an inclined passage which leads to an old gateway, a part of Akbar's buildings. Very little remains of the original buildings which connected it with the palace in the time of Jahângîr, but there cannot be much doubt that this was the locality described by William Finch as the "Dersane Darwaza, leading into a fair court, extending along the river, in which the King looks forth every morning at sun-rising, which he salutes, and then his nobles resort to their

Tesillam (obeisance). Right under the place where he looks out, is a kind of scaffold, whereon his nobles stand, but the *Addis* with others await below in the court. Here also every noone he looketh forth to behold *Tamáshàh*, or fighting of Elephants, Lyons, Buffles, killing of Deare with Leopards, which is a custom on every day of the weeke, Sunday excepted, on which is no fighting; but Tuesday on the contrary, is a day of blood, both of fighting beasts, and justiced men, the King judging and seeing executions."

The Dîwân-i-âm.

The road now turns towards the right, through the Mîna Bazar, the old market-place, where merchants displayed jewellery, brocades, and similar stuffs for the nobles and others attending the court. A gateway leads into the great courtyard of the Dîwân-i-âm, or Hall of Public Audience which, with its surrounding arcades, was for a long time used as an armoury for the British garrison. The hall itself was restored in 1876 by Sir John Strachey, then Lieutenant-Governor of the North-West Provinces. The courtyard has recently been put back, as far as possible, into its original condition by Lord Curzon's orders. A further great improvement has been made by the removal of the hideous modern additions which entirely concealed all the arcades.

The present hall, which is an open pavilion formed by a triple row of colonnades, was commenced by Shah Jahân, but, if we may believe tradition, was not completed until the 27th year of the reign of Aurangzîb. The arcades surrounding the quadrangle are probably of Akbar's time. The interior dimensions of the hall are 192 feet by 64 feet. It is constructed of red sandstone, plastered over with a fine white polished stucco, which served both as a protection to the stone and as a ground for coloured decoration and gilding. This plaster-work was carried to the perfection of a fine art by the old Hindu and Mogul builders; it is still commonly practised in Rajputana and the Punjab.

The throne of the Emperor was in an alcove of inlaid marble at the back of the hall, and connected with the royal apartments behind. Here he sat daily to give audience to his court, to receive ambassadors, and to administer justice. At the foot of the alcove is a square slab of marble, about 3 feet in height, on which, it is said, his ministers stood to receive petitions to the Emperor, and to convey his commands thereon. On the right and left of the throne are chambers with perforated marble windows, through which the ladies of the zanana could view the proceedings. Bernier's.

lively description, though it properly belongs to the Dîwân-i-âm at Delhi, will enable us to picture the scene in the days of the Great Mogul:—

"The monarch every day, about noon, sits upon his throne, with some of his sons at his right and left, while eunuchs standing about the royal person flap away the flies with peacocks' tails, agitate the air with large fans, or wait with undivided attention and profound humility to perform the different services allotted to each. Immediately under the throne is an enclosure, surrounded by silver rails, in which are assembled the whole body of *omrahs* (nobles), the Rajas, and the ambassadors, all standing, their eyes bent downwards and their hands crossed. At a greater distance from the throne are the *mansebdhars*, or inferior *omrahs*, also standing in the same posture of profound reverence. The remainder of the spacious room, and, indeed, the whole courtyard is filled with persons of all ranks, high and low, rich and poor; because it is in this extensive hall that the King gives audience indiscriminately to all his subjects; hence it is called *Am Khas*, or audience chamber of high and low.

"During the hour and a half, or two hours, that this ceremony continues, a certain number of the royal horses pass before the throne, that the King may see whether they are well used and in a proper condition. The elephants come next, their filthy hides having been well washed and painted black as ink, with two large red streaks from the top of the head down to the trunk, where they meet. The elephants are covered with embroidered cloth; a couple of silver-white cow-tails from Great Tibet, of large value, hang from their ears like immense whiskers. Two small elephants, superbly caparisoned, walk close to these colossal creatures, like slaves appointed to their service. As if proud of his gorgeous attire and of the magnificence which surrounds him, every elephant moves with a solemn and dignified step, and, when in front of the throne, the driver, who is seated on his shoulder, pricks him with a pointed iron, animates and speaks to him, until the animal bends one knee, lifts his trunk on high, and roars aloud, which the people consider as the elephants' mode of performing the *taslim*, or usual reverence.

"Other animals are next introduced—tame antelopes, kept for the purpose of fighting with each other; nilgaux, or grey oxen, that appear to me to be a species of elk; rhinoceroses; large Bengale buffaloes, with prodigious horns which enable them to contend against lions and tigers; tame leopards, or panthers, employed in hunting antelopes; some of the fine sporting dogs from

Usbec, of every kind, and each dog with a small red covering; lastly, every species of the birds of prey used in field sports for catching partridges, cranes, hares, and even, it is said, for hunting antelopes, on which they pounce with violence, beating their heads and blinding them with their wings and claws."

After this parade, the more serious business of the day was attended to. The Emperor reviewed his cavalry with peculiar attention, for he was personally acquainted with every trooper. Then all the petitions held up in the assembled crowd were read and disposed of before the audience closed.

On festivals or other special occasions the pillars of the hall were hung with gold brocades, and flowered satin canopies fastened with red silken cords were raised over the whole apartment. The floor was covered entirely with the most magnificent silk carpets. A gorgeous tent, larger than the hall, to which it was fastened, and supported by poles overlaid with silver, was pitched outside. Every compartment of the arcades round the courtyard was decorated by one of the great nobles, at his own expense, with gold brocades and costly carpets, each one vying with the other to attract the attention of the Emperor, to whom, on such occasions, an offering of gold or jewels, more or less valuable according to the pay and rank of the giver, must be presented.

JAHÂNGÎR'S CISTERN.—Just in front of the Dîwân-i-âm is a great stone cistern, cut out of a single block, with steps inside and out, known as Jahângîr's *Hauz*, a bowl or bath-tub. There is a long Persian inscription round the outer rim; the only part now decipherable shows that it was made for Jahângîr in 1019 A.H. (A.D. 1611). It is nearly 5 feet in height and 8 feet in diameter at the top. Its original place is said to have been one of the courts of the Jahangîrî Mahall.

THE TOMB OF MR. COLVIN.—Close by Jahângîr's *Hauz* is the grave of Mr. John Russell Colvin, the Lieutenant-Governor of the North-West Provinces, who died in the Fort during the disturbances of 1857.

The Inner Mîna Bazar.

Before entering the private apartments of the palace, which are at the back of the Dîwân-i-âm, we may pass through the gateway on the left of the courtyard, and enter a smaller one, which was the private bazar where merchants sold jewellery, silks, and costly brocades to the ladies of the zanana, who were seated in the marble balcony which overlooks it (Plate IV.). A narrow staircase gave access to the balcony from the courtyard.

We may well believe that a considerable part of the ladies' time was spent in this quarter of the palace. Sometimes the Great Mogul and his court would amuse themselves by holding a mock fair in which the prettiest of the nobles' wives and daughters would act as traders, and the Emperors and the Begums would bargain with them in the most approved bazar fashion. The Emperor would haggle for the value of an anna, and the ladies would feign indignation, scold his Majesty roundly, and tell him to go where he could suit himself better. "The Begums betray, if possible, a still greater anxiety to be served cheaply; high words are heard on every side, and the loud and scurrilous quarrels of the buyers and sellers create a complete farce. But, when at last the bargains are struck, the Begums, as well as the Emperor, pay liberally for their purchases, and often, as if by accident, let slip out of their hands a few gold instead of silver roupies, as a compliment to the fair merchant and her pretty daughter. Thus the scene ends with merry jests and good humour." (Bernier.)

THE CHITOR GATES.—The further corner of this courtyard, on the left, leads to the Chitor gates, the trophies which Akbar placed there as

Johnston and Hoffman, Photo.]

PLATE IV.—MARBLE BALCONY, OVERLOOKING THE INNER MÎNA BAZAR, AGRA FORT.

a memorial of his capture of that great Rajput stronghold in 1657, after a desperate resistance by its gallant defenders. They form the principal entrance to the *Machchî Bhawân*, the great courtyard behind the Dîwân-i-âm, but are generally kept closed.

THE HINDU TEMPLE.—Beyond the Chitor gates you enter into another quadrangle surrounded by arcades, which recalls a different chapter in the chequered history of the palace. Here is a Hindu temple, built by one of the Bharatpur Rajahs, who sacked Agra about the middle of the 18th century, and occupied it for ten years.

The Machchî Bhawân.

Returning now to the Dîwân-i-âm, we can ascend by one of the small staircases to the throne-room, and enter the upper arcades which surround the Machchî Bhawân, or "Fish Square." The courtyard has suffered so much from ruthless vandalism that it is difficult to realize its former magnificence. It was formerly laid out in marble with flower-beds, water-channels, fountains, and fish-tanks. These were carried off by the Jâts to the palace of Sûraj Mall, at Dîg. A large quantity of mosaic and exquisite marble fretwork, from this and other parts of the palace, was put up to auction by Lord William Bentinck, when Governor-General of India. The Taj only escaped the same fate because the proceeds of this sale were unsatisfactory.

On the side opposite to the throne-room is an open terrace, originally roofed over and connected with the Dîwân-i-khâs. This also was dismantled by the Jâts.

THE NAJINA MASJID.—On the left of the throne-room, at the end of the corridor, is a door leading into a small mosque of white marble, built by Aurangzîb for the ladies of the zanana. It is something like the Môtî Masjid, but far inferior in design.

The further corner of it opens into a small chamber, overlooking the courtyard of the Dîwân-i-âm, which is pointed out by the guides as the prison where Shah Jahân was confined. This may be accepted or not, according to the choice of the visitor. When distinct historical authority is wanting, it is very difficult to distinguish real tradition and pure fable in the tales of these garrulous folk. The historical evidence seems to show that Shah Jahân was not kept a close prisoner, but simply confined to certain apartments in the palace.

We will now pass over to the river side of the

Machchî Bhawân, and approach that part of the palace which contains the Dîwân-i-khâs, or Hall of Private Audience, the Zanana and Mahall-i-khâs, all built by Shah Jahân and occupied by him in the days of his royal state and sovereignty. They rank with the Dîwân-i-khâs at Delhi as the most exquisite of Shah Jahân's buildings. From this classification I purposely omit the Taj, gleaming on the banks of the river lower down. The Taj stands by itself.

The Dîwân-i-Khâs.

The Dîwân-i-khâs was built in 1637. Though much smaller than the Dîwân-i-khâs at Delhi, it is certainly not inferior in the beauty of its proportions and decoration. Most of the decorative work of these marble pavilions is directly derived from Persian art, and inspired by the Persian love of flowers which almost amounted to flower-worship. All the details are charming, but the dados, especially, edged with inlaid work and carved with floral types in the most delicate relief, show to perfection that wonderful decorative instinct which seems to be born in the Oriental handicraftsman. The designer has naïvely translated into marble the conventional Indian flower-beds, just as they were in every palace garden, but there is perfect art in the seeming absence of all artifice. The dados outside the Taj are similar in design to these, though larger and correspondingly bolder in style. The roof of the Dîwân-i-khâs, with its fine coved ceiling, is interesting for its construction.

JAHÂNGÎR'S THRONE.—On the terrace in front of the Dîwân-i-khâs are placed two thrones, one of white marble on the side facing the Machchî-Bhawân, and the other of black slate on the river side. From the Persian inscription which runs round the four sides of the black throne we learn that it was made in 1603 for Jahângîr. This was two years before the death of his father, Akbar, and he was then only Prince Salîm. The throne was, therefore, probably made to commemorate the recognition by Akbar of his son's title to the succession.

On this terrace Jahângîr sat to enjoy the sight of his brigantines on the river, or to watch the elephant fights on the level place beneath the walls. From side to side of his throne there is a long fissure, which opened, so says tradition, when the Jât Rajah, Jawahar Singh of Bharatpur, in 1765, set his usurping feet on the throne of the Great Mogul. The tradition holds that blood spurted out of the throne in two places, and red

Johnston and Hoffman, Photo.]

PLATE V.—THE SAMMAN BURJ, AGRA FORT.

marks in the stone are pointed out as evidence of the truth of the story. The impious chief was shortly afterwards assassinated in the palace.

THE BATHS.—On the side of the terrace directly opposite to the Dîwân-i-khâs are the baths, or the Hammâm. The water was brought up from a well, outside the walls, 70 feet below. These baths, in their present state, are by no means so fine as those at Fatehpur Sîkrî, to be described hereafter.

The Marquis of Hastings, when Governor-General of India, broke up one of the most beautiful of the baths of the palace, and sent it home as a present to the Prince Regent, afterwards George the Fourth.

The Samman Burj.

A doorway at the back of the Dîwân-i-khâs leads to the beautiful two-storied pavilion, surmounting one of the most projecting of the circular bastions on the river face, and known as the Samman Burj, "the Jasmine Tower" (Plate V.). The style of the inlaid work shows it to be earlier in date than the Dîwân-i-khâs, and supports Fergusson's conjecture that it was built by Jahângîr. In that case it must have been the apartment of his Empress, the beautiful and accomplished

Nûr Mahall. It was afterwards occupied by Mumtâz Mahall, the lady of the Taj. Here, also, in full view of the famous monument he had raised to her memory, died her husband, Shah Jahân—sensualist, perhaps, but true to his last hours to one great master-passion. The faithful Jahânârâ who shared his captivity for seven years, attended him on his death-bed, and, as the shades of night closed in and hid the Taj from view—praying Divine forgiveness for his sins, and with a few consoling words to his daughter—he went to join his beloved!

After the rites prescribed by the Muhammadan law, the body was placed in a coffin of sandal-wood and conveyed by the passage which leads from the Samman Burj to the low gate beneath it, which was specially opened for the occasion. Thence, followed by a procession of mourners, it was carried out of the Fort through the Shêr Hâji gate, nearly opposite (now closed), and conveyed across the arm of the river to its last resting-place in the Taj.

The death of Shah Jahân and his funeral are minutely described by Mulla Muhammad Kâzim in his "Alamgir Nâma." The guides wrongly point out a pavilion in the Jahângîrî Mahall as the place where he died.

In front of the Samman Burj is a beautiful

little fountain hollowed in the floor; on one side of the courtyard is a raised platform laid out in squares of black marble for the game of *pachîsî*, an Eastern backgammon.[1]

The Khâs Mahall.

From the Samman Burj we step into the next set of apartments of the zanana, connecting with the Khâs Mahall and a similar set on the other side. This part of the zanana forms the east, or riverside, of the Angûrî Bagh, or Grape Garden. There is an indescribable grace and charm about all this quarter of the palace, to which the beauty of the material, the perfect taste of the ornament and elegance of the proportions, the delightful background of the landscape, and the historical associations all contribute. It should be seen towards evening, not in the full glare of the morning sun.

When the afterglow fills the sky, burnishes the gilded roofs, and turns the marble to rose-colour, imagination may re-people these lovely pavilions with fair Indian women—revel in the

[1] An ugly modern marble rail, in imitation of wood, probably a reminiscence of the time when the palace was occupied by the British garrison, still disfigures and stunts the proportions of the upper storey of the Samman Burj.

feast of colour in *saris*, brocades, and carpets; in the gold, azure, and crimson of the painted ceilings; and listen to the water splashing in the fountains and gurgling over the carved water-shoots—a scene of voluptuous beauty such as the world has rarely known since the wealth and elegance of Rome filled the palaces and villas of Pompei.

In the walls of the Khâs Mahall are a number of niches which formerly contained portraits of the Mogul Emperors, beginning with Tîmûr, which, like so many other things, were looted by the Rajah of Bharatpur. A number of similar portraits and other fine paintings of the Mogul period are preserved in the Government Art Gallery, Calcutta.

A Persian poem inscribed on the walls of the Khâs Mahall gives the date of its construction, 1636.

THE UNDERGROUND CHAMBERS.—A staircase to the south of the Khâs Mahall leads to a labyrinth of underground chambers, in which the Emperor and his zanana found refuge from the fierce summer heat of Agra. In the south-east corner there is a well-house, called a *bâoli;* this is a set of chambers surrounding a well—a favourite retreat in the hot weather. There were formerly many of the kind round about Agra, constructed by the Mogul Emperors or their nobles. Besides these resorts of ease and pleasure, there are gloomy dungeons which tell of misbehaving slaves and indiscreet sultanas, who were hurried down to meet their fate at the hands of the executioner, the silent Jumna receiving their lifeless bodies.

The Angûrî Bâgh.

The great quadrangle in front of the Khâs Mahall is the Angûrî Bâgh, surrounded on three sides by arcades, probably built by Akbar and intended for his zanana. They were occupied in the Mutiny days by the British officers and their families who were shut up in the Fort.

The Angûrî Bâgh is a very typical specimen of the old Mogul gardens, laid out in geometrical flower-beds, with four terraced walks radiating from the central platform and fountain. A stone trellis which formerly enclosed the flower-beds, and probably supported the vines which gave the garden its name has lately been restored.

Among the many improvements made by Lord Curzon in the Fort was the clearance of the wire-netting fernhouses and bedraggled shrubs which formerly disfigured the quadrangle. If it cannot be kept up in the old Mogul style, it is certainly better to leave the garden uncultivated.

Shîsh Mahall.—On the north side of the Angûrî

Bâgh, close to the zanana, a passage leads to the *Shîsh Mahall*, or "palace of glass." This was the bath of the zanana. The marble slabs of the floor have been torn up, and the decoration with a kind of glass mosaic seems to have suffered from clumsy attempts at renovation. A passage from the Shîsh Mahall leads to the old water gate.

THE "SOMNATH" GATES.—Before entering the Jahângîrî Mahal, on the opposite side of the Angûrî Bâgh, we will pause at a corner of the zanana courtyard, where a small apartment contains an interesting relic of the Afghan expedition of 1842—the so-called "Somnath" gates, taken from the tomb of Mahmûd of Ghazni in the capture of that city by the British. They were the subject of a most extraordinary archæological blunder by the Governor-General, Lord Ellenborough, who, in a grandiloquent proclamation, identifying them with the gates of carved sandalwood which Mahmûd, according to tradition, had taken from the celebrated Hindu temple of Somnath in 1025, announced to the people of India that "the insult of eight hundred years had been avenged." The gates were conveyed on a triumphal car through the towns of Northern India to the Agra Fort, and deposited there with great ceremony. As a matter of fact, the wood is deodar, and not sandalwood, and from the style of the ornament there can be hardly a doubt that the gates were made at or near Ghazni. One glance would convince any expert in Oriental archæology that they could not by any possibility have been the gates of a Hindu temple.

It has been supposed that the original gates were destroyed by fire, and that these were made to replace them, but there seems to be considerable doubt whether Mahmûd really took away any gates from the Somnath temple. It certainly would have been unusual for the great Muhammadan plunderer to have burdened himself with an archæological relic which, in those days, was not easily convertible into cash.

A horse-shoe which is nailed to the gate is not, as is generally supposed, a propitiation of the Goddess of Fortune, but a token from the owner of some sick animal that he would bring an offering to the shrine in the event of a cure resulting from his visit. This was an old custom among the Tartars and other nomad tribes, who valued horses and cattle as their most precious possessions.

The Jahângîrî Mahall.

The palace called after Jahângîr, the Jahângîrî Mahall, is in many respects the most remarkable building of its class in India. Nothing could be more striking than the contrast between the extreme elegance, bordering on effeminacy, of the marble pavilions of Shah Jahân's palaces, and the robust, virile, yet highly imaginative architecture of this palace of Akbar; for though it bears Jahângîr's name there cannot be much doubt that it was planned, and partially, if not completely, carried out by Akbar with the same architects who built Fatehpur Sîkrî. It is the perfected type of the style which we see in process of evolution at Fatehpur, and were it not for the Taj, we might regret the new element which came into Mogul architecture with Itmâd-ud-daulah's tomb. Both of these styles, which appear side by side in the Agra Fort, are intensely typical of the men and the times which produced them. The one is stamped throughout with the personality of Akbar the empire-builder, and distinguished by the stately solidity of Hindu architecture. In the other the native vigour of the earlier Indian styles has been softened by the cultured eclecticism of Persia and Arabia, for the manly dignity of Akbar's court had given place to the sensual luxury of Shah Jahân's

On the river side of the palace there is an octagonal pavilion placed similarly to the Samman

Burj, which is very charming in its fresco decoration, though the colour has faded very much. It is possibly this pavilion to which Badâyunî, one of Akbar's biographers, refers when he describes a Brahmin, named Dêbi, being pulled up the walls of the castle, sitting on a *charpâi* (a native bed), till he arrived near the balcony where the Emperor used to sleep. "Whilst thus suspended he instructed his Majesty in the secrets and legends of Hinduism, in the manner of worshipping idols, the fire, the sun, and stars, and of revering the chief gods of these unbelievers." The priests of other religions were similarly carried up to converse with Akbar.

Adjoining this is a set of small rooms, known as Akbar's apartments, which, even in their present dilapidated state, show that they must have possessed a richness and beauty of decoration inferior to nothing else in the whole Fort. The dados were decorated with *gesso* work on a gold ground. The borders are still almost intact, but the rest of the relief ornament seems to have been wantonly hacked off out of pure mischief. I believe this is the only example of *gesso* work in any of Akbar's buildings. The treatment of the upper part of the walls with the characteristic cuspings of Arabian and Moorish architects is admirable.

Passing through these, we enter a long room know as the library, in which a not very successful attempt was made some years ago to restore the painted decoration. It is to be devoutly hoped that this and other dangerous experiments of the kind will not be continued, except under skilled artistic supervision. The restoration of the structural parts of the palace and of the stone carving is a more easy matter, for the descendants of the very men who built and carved the palace still practise their art in Agra and round about. This has been admirably carried out by the Public Works Department under Lord Curzon's orders.

The outer courtyard, on the riverside, is very interesting, especially for a very elegant and original porch, in which Saracenic feeling predominates; but on entering the inner courtyard (Plate VI.) it is more easy to realize that this palace is one of the great masterpieces of Mogul architecture. The beauty of this inner quadrangle is derived not so much from its fine proportions and rich ornamentation as from the wonderful rhythmic play of light and shadow, produced by the bracket form of construction and the admirable disposition of the openings for doors, windows, and colonnades. The north side of the quadrangle is formed by a pillared hall, of distinctly Hindu

PLATE VI.—INNER COURTYARD OF THE JAHÂNGÎRÎ MAHALL, AGRA FORT.

design, full of the feeling of mystery characteristic of indigenous Indian styles. The subdued light of the interior adds to the impressiveness of its great piers stretching their giant brackets up to the roof like the gnarled and twisted branches of primeval forest trees. A very interesting point of view can be obtained from the gallery which runs round the upper part of the hall.

One of Jahângîr's wives, a Hindu princess of Jodhpur, hence known as Jodh Bai, lived in this part of the palace, and the room on the west side of the quadrangle, surrounded by a number of oblong niches, is said to have been her temple, in which the images of Hanuman and other Hindu deities were kept.

On the roof of the Jahângîrî Mahall there are two fine pavilions; also a number of cisterns, which supplied the palace with water. In the side of one of them there are a number of pipe-holes, lined with copper, over each of which is a circular stone label inscribed with the part of the palace to which it gave a supply.

The Salîmgarh.

On the rising ground behind the courtyard of the Dîwân-i-âm there formerly existed a palace called the Salîmgarh. Before Jahângîr's accession he was known as Prince Salîm, and tradition associates this palace with him. Fergusson, however, states that in his time an exquisite fragment of a palace built by Shêr Shah, or his son Salîm, existed here. The Salîmgarh at Delhi is named after the son of Shêr Shah, Salîm Shah Sûr, who built it, and there is some doubt as to which of the two Salîms gave his name to the Salîmgarh at Agra. Akbar's Fort is known to have been built to replace an older one (known as the Badalgarh) by Salîm Shah Sûr, but it is quite possible that a part of the palace may have been left, and retained the name of its founder.

The only part of the Salîmgarh which now remains is a large two-storied pavilion in front of the barracks. The upper half of the exterior is carved with extraordinary richness. The style of design certainly indicates the period of the Jahângîrî Mahall and Akbar's buildings at Fatehpur Sîkrî, rather than Shêr Shah's work.

The Jâm'i Masjid.

Nearly opposite to the Delhi Gate of the Fort is the Jâm'i Masjid, or Cathedral Mosque, built by Jahânara, Shah Jahân's eldest daughter. It is in the same style as the splendid mosque built by Shah Jahân at Delhi, but far inferior in merit.

There is a tameness about the whole design very unusual in the buildings of this epoch. The zig-zag striping of the domes is decidedly unpleasant.

An inscription over the main archway states that it was completed in the year 1644 A.D., at a cost of five lakhs of rupees.

THE TAJ

ARJUMAND BÂNÛ BEGAM, the favourite wife of Shah Jahân, is better known by her other name, Mumtâz Mahall ("the Crown of the Palace"). Her father was Âsaf Khan, who was brother of the Empress Nûr Mahall, Jahângîr's wife. She was thus the granddaughter of Itmâd-ud-daulah, Jahângîr's Prime Minister, whose tomb, on the opposite bank of the river, will be described hereafter.

In 1612, at the age of nineteen years she was married to Shah Jahân—then Prince Khurram—who, though hardly twenty-one, had already another wife. This second marriage, however, was a real love-match, and Mumtâz was her husband's inseparable companion on all his journeys and military expeditions. Shah Jahân, like his father, allowed his wife a large share in the responsibilities of government. Like Nûr Mahall, she was famed as much for her charity as for her beauty. Her influence was especially exercised in obtaining clemency for criminals condemned to death. She bore him fourteen children, and died in childbed in 1631, or the fourth year after Shah Jahân's accession to the throne, at Burhânpur, whither she had accompanied her husband on a campaign against Khân Jahân Lodi. The Emperor was overpowered with grief. For a week he refused to see any of his ministers, or to transact any business of state. He even contemplated resigning the throne and dividing the empire among his sons. For two years the court observed strict mourning. No music or festivities were allowed; the wearing of jewels, the use of perfumes and luxuries of all kinds were forbidden. The month of Zikad, in which she died, was observed as a month of mourning for many years afterwards. The body of Mumtâz was removed to Agra, and remained temporarily in the garden of the Taj while the foundations of the building were being laid. It was then placed in the vault where it now lies. A temporary dome covered the tomb while the great monument grew up over it.

The building of the Taj.

It was one of those intervals in history when the whole genius of a people ins concentrated on great architectural works, and art becomes an epitome of the age. For the Taj was not a creation of a single master-mind, but the consummation of a great art epoch. Since the time of Akbár the best architects, artists, and art workmen of India, Persia, Arabia, and Central Asia had been attracted to the Mogul court. All the resources of a great empire were at their disposal, for Shah Jahân desired that this monument of his grief should be one of the wonders of the world. The sad circumstances which attended the early death of the devoted wife who had endeared herself to the people might well inspire all his subjects to join in the Emperor's pious intentions.

According to the old Tartar custom, a garden was chosen as a site for the tomb—a garden planted with flowers and flowering shrubs, the emblems of life, and solemn cypress, the emblem of death and eternity. Such a garden, in the Mogul days, was kept up as a pleasure-ground during the owner's lifetime, and used as his last resting-place after his death. The old tradition laid down that it must be acquired by fair means, and not by force or fraud. So Rajah Jey Singh, to whom the garden belonged, was compensated by the gift of another property from the Emperor's private estate. Shah Jahân next appointed a council of the best architects of his empire for preparing the design for the building. Drawings of many of the most celebrated buildings of the world were shown and discussed. It is even believed that one Geronimo Veroneo, an Italian who was then in the Mogul service, submitted designs for Shah Jahân's inspection, a fact which has led many writers into the error of supposing that the Taj, as completed, was actually designed by him.[1] The design eventually accepted was by Ustâd Îsâ, who is stated in one account to have come from *Rûm* (Asiatic Turkey), and in another to have been a native of Shiraz, in Persia.

The master-builders came from many different parts; the chief masons from Baghdad, Delhi, and Multân; the dome builders from Asiatic Turkey and from Samarkand; the inlay workers from Kanauj and from Baghdad; the principal calligraphist for the inscriptions from Shiraz. Every part of India and Central Asia contributed the materials: Jaipur, the marble; Fatehpur Sîkrî, the red sandstone; the Panjab, jasper; China, the jade and crystal; Tibet, turquoises; Ceylon, lapis lazuli and sapphires; Arabia, coral and cornelian; Panna in Bundelkund, diamonds; Persia, onyx and amethyst. Twenty thousand men were employed in the construction, which took seventeen years to complete.[2] The cenotaph was originally

[1] See Appendix for a full discussion of this interesting question.

[2] Tavernier says twenty-two years, probably including all the accessory buildings.

Johnston and Hoffman, Photo.]

PLATE VII.—MARBLE SCREEN ENCLOSING THE TOMBS OF MUMTÂZ MAHALL AND SHAH JAHÂN.

enclosed by a fence or screen of gold studded with gems. This was removed in 1642, and replaced by the present exquisite screen of pierced marble (Plate VII.). The Taj also possessed formerly two wonderful silver doors. Austin de Bordeaux, a French goldsmith, who was employed by Shah Jahân in making the celebrated Peacock Throne, may possibly have executed some of this metal-work in the Taj; but there is no evidence worthy of consideration to support the common Anglo-Indian belief that he designed or superintended the *pietra dura*, or inlaid marble decoration of the building, which is entirely of the Persian school.[1] These silver doors were looted and melted down by the Jâts in 1764.

Besides the lavish expenditure on the building, lakhs of rupees were spent in providing the richest of Persian silk carpets, golden lamps, and magnificent candlesticks. A sheet of pearls, valued at several lakhs, was made to cover the sarcophagus. This was carried off by the Amir Husein Ali Khan, in 1720, as part of his share of the spoil of Agra. The total expenditure, according to the highest estimates, amounted to over 400 lakhs of rupees.

It is said that Shah Jahân had intended to construct a mausoleum for himself opposite to the Taj, on the other side of the Jumnâ, and

[1] See Appendix I.

to connect the two by a great bridge. The project was interrupted and never completed, owing to the usurpation of Aurangzîb, shortly after the foundations were laid.

The Intention of the Taj.

The Taj has been the subject of numberless critical essays, but many of them have missed the mark entirely, because the writers have not been sufficiently conversant with the spirit of Eastern artistic thought. All comparisons with the Parthenon or other classic buildings are useless. One cannot compare Homer with the Mahâbhârata, or Kalidâs with Euripides. The Parthenon was a temple for Pallas Athene, an exquisite casket to contain the jewel. The Taj is the jewel—the ideal itself. Indian architecture is in much closer affinity to the great conceptions of the Gothic builders than it is to anything of classic or Renaissance construction. The Gothic cathedral, with its sculptured arches and its spires pointing heavenwards, is a symbol, as most Eastern buildings are symbols. The Mogul artists, being prevented by the precepts of the Muhammadan religion from attempting sculpture, as understood in Europe, succeeded in investing their great architectural monuments with an extraordinary personal character. There is a wonderful personality in the dignity and greatness of Akbar's tomb; we see the scholar and the polished courtier in Itmâd-ud-daulah's. But the Taj carries this idea of personality further than had been attempted in any of the Mogul monuments; it represents in art the highest development towards individualism, the struggle against the restraints of ritualism and dogma, which Akbar initiated in religion.

Every one who has seen the Taj must have felt that there is something in it, difficult to define or analyze, which differentiates it from all other buildings in the world. Sir Edwin Arnold has struck the true note of criticism in the following lines :—

> " Not Architecture ! as all others are,
> But the proud passion of an emperor's love
> Wrought into living stone, which gleams and soars
> With body of beauty shrining soul and thought ;
> . . . As when some face
> Divinely fair unveils before our eyes—
> Some woman beautiful unspeakably—
> And the blood quickens, and the spirit leaps,
> And will to worship bends the half-yielded knees
> While breath forgets to breathe. So is the Taj !"

This is not a mere flight of poetic fancy, but a deep and true interpretation of the meaning of the Taj. What were the thoughts of the designers, and of Shah Jahân himself, when they resolved to raise a monument of eternal love to the Crown of the Palace—Taj Mahall ? Surely not only of a mausoleum—a sepulchre fashioned after ordinary architectural canons, but of an architectonic ideal, symbolical of her womanly grace and beauty. Those critics who have objected to the effeminacy of the architecture unconsciously pay the highest tribute to the genius of the builders. The Taj was meant to be feminine. The whole conception, and every line and detail of it, express the intention of the designers. It is Mumtâz Mahall herself, radiant in her youthful beauty, who still lingers on the banks of the shining Jumnâ, at early morn, in the glowing midday sun, or in the silver moonlight. Or rather, we should say, it conveys a more abstract thought; it is India's noble tribute to the grace of Indian womanhood—the Venus de Milo of the East.

Bearing this in mind, we can understand how foolish it is to formulate criticisms of the Taj based on ordinary architectural principles as practised in Europe. Many of these criticisms, which might be appropriate enough if applied to a modern provincial town hall, are only silly and impertinent in reference to the Taj. Some are born tone-deaf, others colour-blind, and there are many who can find beauty in one particular form or expression of art and in no others. So the Taj will always find detractors. But whoever tries to understand the imaginative side of Eastern thought will leave the critics to themselves, and take unrestrained delight in the exquisitely subtle rhythm of this marvellous creation of Mogul art.

As one approaches the Taj from the west, and before entering the quadrangle in front of the gateway, attention should be given to a fine little building on the right called the Sahelî Burj, which is one of four monuments erected in memory of maids of honour in the service of Mumtâz Mahall. It was formerly in a very dilapidated and neglected state: its restoration to its present condition is one of the many admirable works of the kind carried out by the Archæological Survey of India, under the direction of Mr. J. H. Marshall, C.I.E., in Lord Curzon's Viceroyalty. Mr. Marshall says truly of these four buildings, that in any other place, where they were not overshadowed by the beauty of the Taj, they might well attract more attention than they usually receive, for their design is very interesting, and they all belong to the best period of Mogul architecture.

The gateway of the Taj faces a spacious quadrangle surrounded by arcades. This is a *caravan serai*, or place where travellers halted. Here, also, the poor were provided with food and shelter, and on the anniversary day vast sums were distributed in charity from the funds with which the Taj was endowed. It is well to pause before entering, and admire the proportions and perfect taste of the decoration of this gateway; for afterwards one has no eyes for anything but the Taj itself. It is much finer in design than the similar gateway of Akbar's tomb at Sikandra. An Arabic inscription in black marble, of passages taken from the Koran, frames the principal arch, and invites the pure of heart to enter the Gardens of Paradise.

The first view of the Taj is from within this noble portal, framed by the sombre shadow of the great arch which opens on to the garden. At the end of a long terrace, its gracious outline partly mirrored in the still water of a wide canal, a fairy vision of silver-white—like the spirit of purity—seems to rest so lightly, so tenderly, on the earth, as if in a moment it would soar into the sky. The beauty of the Taj, as in all great art, lies in its simplicity. One wonders that so much beauty can come from so little effort. Yet nothing is wanting, nothing in excess; one cannot alter this and that and say that it is better.

The garden, as originally planned, was an integral part of one great design. The solemn rows of cypresses were planted so as to help out the lines of the architecture; the flowering trees and flower-beds completed the harmony with a splendid glow of colour.[1] Beautiful as the first view of the Taj is even now, one can hardly realize how glorious it must have been when the whole intention of the design was fulfilled. At present there is not a single spot in the garden itself which gives a view of the composition as a whole.

Advancing down the main terrace, paved with stone and laid out with geometric flower-beds, we reach a marble platform with its fountain (see frontispiece),[2] where a nearer view of the Taj may be enjoyed. Such a platform was the central feature in all Mogul gardens. The terraces to the right and left of it end in two fine pavilions of red sandstone, intended for the accommodation of the custodians of the mausoleum and for storehouses.

From this point we can admire the effect of the exquisite inlaid decoration, fine and precious as the embroidery on the raiment of Mumtâz herself. At the end of the main terrace we reach

[1] The garden as it existed in 1904 was a jungle planted by a European overseer without any understanding or feeling for the ideas of the Mogul artists. The overgrown trees entirely blocked out the view of the mosques on either side, which are an essential part of the whole composition, serving as supporters to the slender detached minarets. Since then some of the more obstructive of the larger trees have been removed; but the avenue of cypress trees, which perished from drought some years ago, has been replanted on lines which eventually will clash seriously with the architectural composition.

[2] This represents the condition of the garden thirty or forty years ago.

the steps leading up to the great platform on which the Taj and its minarets, "four tall court ladies tending their Princess," are raised.

Let us reverently enter the central chamber, where Mumtâz Mahall and Shah Jahân, her lord and lover, lie. Fergusson has truly said, no words can express its chastened beauty seen in the soft gloom of the subdued light coming from the distant and half-closed openings. The screen of marble tracery which surrounds the tombs is in itself a masterpiece. Even with all the artistic resources which Shah Jahân had at his command, it was a work of ten years. Mumtâz Mahall lies in the centre. The white marble of her tomb blossoms with a never-fading garden of Persian flowers, which the magic of the Mogul artists has created.

The inscription on it is as follows: "The illustrious sepulchre of Arjumand Bânû Begam, called Mumtâz Mahall. Died in 1040 A.H." (1631 A.D.).

At the head of the cenotaph is the line: "He is the everlasting: He is sufficient;" and the following passage from the Koran: "God is He, besides whom there is no God. He knoweth what is concealed and what is manifest. He is merciful and compassionate."

On one side of it: "Nearer unto God are those who say 'Our Lord is God.'"

The inscription on the cenotaph of Shah Jahân

is as follows: "The illustrious sepulchre and sacred resting-place of His Most Exalted Majesty dignified as Razwan (the guardian of Paradise), having his abode in Paradise, and his dwelling in the starry heaven, inhabitant of the regions of bliss, the second lord of the Qirán,[1] Shah Jahân, the king valiant. May his tomb ever flourish, and may his abode be in the heavens. He travelled from this transitory world to the world of eternity on the night of the 28th of the month of Rajab, 1076 A.H." (1666 A.D.).

The sarcophagi containing the remains of Shah Jahân and his wife are immediately under these cenotaphs, in the vault below. Not the least of the wonders of this wonderful building is in its acoustic qualities. It does not respond to vulgar noises, but if a few notes be slowly and softly sung in this vault, and especially if the chord of the seventh be sounded, they are caught up by the echoes of the roof and repeated in endless harmonies, which seem to those listening above as if a celestial choir were chanting angelic hymns. "It haunts the air above and around; it distils in showers upon the polished marble; it rises, it falls. . . . It is the very element with which sweet

[1] The conjunction of Jupiter and Venus; referring to the circumstance that Tîmûr and himself were born at the conjunction of these planets. (KEENE.)

dreams are builded. It is the spirit of the Taj, the voice of inspired love!"

Surrounding the central chamber are eight smaller ones for the mullahs who chanted the Koran and for musicians who played soft Indian and Persian melodies. The vault below was only opened once a year, on the anniversary day, when the Emperor and all his court attended a solemn festival. Even on ordinary occasions none but Muhammadans were admitted into the interior. Bernier tells us that he had not seen it, on that account, but he understood that nothing could be conceived more rich and magnificent.

The two mosques of red sandstone on either side of the Taj are in the same style as the entrance gateway, the interiors being decorated with fresco and fine cut plaster-work. The one towards the west was intended for prayers only; the floor is panelled into separate spaces for each worshipper. The opposite mosque was known as the *Jamaat Khâna*, or meeting-place for the congregation before prayers, and on the occasion of the great anniversary service. Standing on the platform in front of this mosque, one has a splendid view of the Taj, the river, and the distant Fort.

As the garden is now arranged, a full view of the magnificent platform, with its two mosques, and the Taj itself, can only be obtained from the opposite side of the river, which is not very accessible except by boat. When the traveller leaves Agra by rail, going east, the Taj in all its glory can be seen in the distance, floating like the mirage of some wondrous fairy palace over the waving tufts of the pampas grass, until at last it sinks into the pale horizon.

NOTE.—A small museum has been established lately by the Archæological Department, in the western half of the Taj main gateway. It contains an interesting collection of photographs and drawings of the Taj at different periods, and specimens of the stones used in the *pietra dura*, or inlay work of the building. There are also samples illustrating the technique of *pietra dura* and the tools used by native workmen.

ITMÂD-UD-DAULAH'S TOMB

THE tomb of Itmâd-ud-daulah, "the Lord High Treasurer," is on the east or left bank of the river, and is reached by crossing the pontoon bridge. It was built by Nûr Mahall, the favourite wife of Jahângîr, as a mausoleum for her father, Mirza Ghias Beg, who, according to one account, was a Persian from Teheran, and by another a native of Western Tartary.

A story is told of the Mirza's early life, of which it can only be said, *Si non è vero è ben trovato.* He left his home, accompanied by his wife and children, to seek his fortune in India, where he had some relatives at Akbar's court. His slender provision for the journey was exhausted in crossing the Great Desert, and they were all in danger of perishing from hunger. In this extremity his wife gave birth to a daughter. The unhappy parents, distracted by hunger and fatigue, left the infant under a solitary shrub. With the father supporting his wife and children on the one bullock which remained to them, they pushed on

Johnston and Hoffman, Photo.]

PLATE VIII.—ITMÂD-UD-DAULAH'S TOMB, AGRA.

in the hope of finding relief; but as the tiny landmark where the infant lay disappeared in the distance, the mother, in a paroxysm of grief, threw herself to the ground, crying, "My child! my child!" The piteous appeal forced the father to return to restore the babe to her mother, and soon afterwards a caravan appeared in sight and rescued the whole party.

The child born under these romantic circumstances became the Empress Nûr Mahall, who built this mausoleum. Her father reached Lahore, where Akbar then held his court, and through the influence of his friends attracted the Emperor's attention. His talents won for him speedy promotion, and under Jahângîr he became first Lord High Treasurer, and afterwards Wazîr, or Prime Minister. Jahângîr, in his memoirs, candidly discusses the character of his father-in-law. He was a good scholar, with a pretty taste for poetry, possessed many social qualities and a genial disposition. His accounts were always in perfect order, but "he liked bribes, and showed much boldness in demanding them." On his death his son, Âsaf Khan, the father of Mumtâz Mahall, was appointed to succeed him.

Itmâd-ud-daulah and his wife are buried in the central chamber; his brother and sister and other members of his family occupy the four corners.

The pavilion on the roof, enclosed by beautiful marble tracery (Plate IX.), contains only replicas of the real tombs beneath. The mausoleum was commenced in 1622 and completed in 1628. As a composition it may lack inspiration, but it is exceedingly elegant, and scholarly like the Lord High Treasurer himself. In construction it marks the transition from the style of Akbar to that of Shah Jahân; from the Jahângîrî Mahall to the Dîwân-i-khâs, the Môtî Masjid, and the Taj. The towers at the four corners might be the first suggestion of the detached minarets of the Taj. The Hindu feeling which is so characteristic of most of Akbar's buildings is here only conspicuous in the roof of the central chamber over the tomb; in pure Saracenic architecture a tomb is always covered by a dome.

This change in style greatly influenced the architecture of the whole of the north of India, Hindu as well as Muhammadan. It must be remembered that comparatively few of the master-builders who actually constructed the most famous examples of Mogul architecture were Muhammadans. The remarkable decline of the Mogul style which set in under Aurangzîb was largely due to his bigotry in refusing to employ any but true believers.

The family ties of Itmâd-ud-daulah and his

daughter, the Empress, were closely connected with Persia and Central Asia; and no doubt the fashion set by Jahângîr's court led to the Saracenic element becoming predominant in the Mogul style both in construction and in decoration. Many authorities have connected the marked difference between Itmâd-ud-daulah's tomb and Akbar's buildings to Italian influence, only on the ground that Jahângîr is known to have been partial to Europeans, and allowed them free access to his palace. There is not, however, a trace of Italian art in any detail of the building; there is not a form or decorative idea which had not been used in India or in Central Asia for centuries. The use of marble inlaid work on so extensive a scale was a novelty, but it was only an imitation, or adaptation, of the splendid tile-mosaic and painted tile-work which were the commonest kinds of decoration employed in Persia: Wazîr Khan's mosque at Lahore, built in Jahângîr's time, is a fine Indian example of the latter.

The art of inlaying stone had been practised in India for many years before this building; but here, for the first time, do we find the inlayers making attempts at direct imitation of Persian pottery decoration. All the familiar *motifs* of Persian art, the tree of life and other floral types, the cypress tree, the flower-vases, fruits, wine-cups, and rose-water vessels are here reproduced exactly as they are found in Persian mosaic tiles. In Shah Jahân's palace and in the Taj they went a step further, and imitated the more naturalistic treatment of Persian fresco painting and other pictorial art; but there is never the slightest suggestion of European design in the decoration of these buildings.

It is quite possible that some Italians may have shown the native inlayers specimens of Florentine *pietra dura*, and suggested to them this naturalistic treatment, but if Italians or other Europeans had been engaged to instruct or supervise in the decoration of these buildings they would certainly have left some traces of their handiwork. In the technical part of the process the Indian workmen had nothing to learn, and in the design they made no attempt to follow European forms, except in the one solitary instance of the decoration of the throne-chamber of the Delhi Palace, which is much later in date than Itmâd-ud-daulah's tomb.[1]

The whole scheme of the exterior decoration is so finely carried out, both in arrangement and colour, that its extreme elaboration produces no effect of unquietness. At a distance it only gives

[1] It is very probable that the black slate or marble panels in the Delhi Palace, which are purely Florentine in design, were imported complete from Italy, and fixed in the wall by Indian workmen, who only designed the ornamental scrolls surrounding the panels.

Johnston and Hoffman, Photo.]

PLATE IX.—INTERIOR OF THE UPPER PAVILION, ITMÂD-UD-DAULAH'S TOMB.

a suggestion of a soft bloom or iridescence on the surface of the marble. The soffits of the doorways are carved with extraordinary delicacy. Inside the building there are remains of fresco and other painted decoration.

Beautifully placed on the river bank, there is a fine little mosque, which at sunset makes a charming picture. The boldness and greater simplicity of the decoration contrast well with the richness of that of the mausoleum.

THE CHÎNI-KÂ-RAUZA

Beyond Itmâd-ud-daulah's tomb, on the same side of the river, is a beautiful ruin, once entirely covered with the same Persian mosaic tile-work, which suggested the more costly style of decoration in inlaid marble. It is called Chînî-kâ-Rauza, or the China Tomb, and is supposed to be the mausoleum of Âfzal Khan, a Persian poet, who entered the service of Jahângîr, and afterwards became Prime Minister to Shah Jahân. He died in Lahore in 1639. The weather and ill-treatment of various kinds have removed a great deal of the exquisite enamel colours from the tiles, but enough remains to indicate how rich and magnificent the effect must have been originally. A part of the south façade which has fallen in shows how the builders employed earthen pots to lessen the weight of the concrete filling, a practice followed in the ancient dome construction of Egypt and Rome.

THE RÂM BAGH

AMONG a number of more or less ruined garden-houses on this bank of the river, there is one, a little beyond the Chînî-kâ-Rauza, of especial interest, on account of the tradition which associates it with the Emperor Bâbar. It is called the Râm Bagh, and is believed to have been one of the "elegant and regularly planned pleasure-grounds" which Bâbar laid out and planted with fruit trees and flowers, as he has described in his memoirs.

No doubt this was the scene of many imperial picnics; not the drunken revels of Bâbar's Kabul days—for just before the great battle with the Rajputs in 1527 he smashed all his gold and silver drinking-cups and took a vow of total abstinence, which he kept faithfully—but the more sane and temperate pleasures which music, poetry, and his intense delight in the beauties of nature could furnish. Here is a charming picture he has given of another garden he laid out in the Istalif district of Kabul:—

"On the outside of the garden are large and

beautiful spreading plane-trees, under the shade of which there are agreeable spots, finely sheltered. A perennial stream, large enough to turn a mill, runs through the garden, and on its banks are planted plane and other trees. Formerly this stream flowed in a winding and crooked course, but I ordered its course to be altered according to a plan which added greatly to the beauty of the place. Lower down . . . on the lower skirts of the hills is a fountain, named Kwâjeh-seh-yârân (Kwâjeh three friends), around which are three species of trees; above the fountain are many beautiful plane trees, which yield a pleasant shade. On the two sides of the fountain, on small eminences at the bottom of the hills, there are a number of oak trees. Except on these two spots, where there are groves of oak, there is not an oak to be met with on the hills of the west of Kabul. In front of this fountain, towards the plain, there are many spots covered with the flowering arghwân tree, and, besides these arghwân plots, there are none else in the whole country. It is said that these three kinds of trees were bestowed on it by the power of these three holy men, beloved of God; and that is the origin of the name Sej-Yârân. I directed this fountain to be built round with stone, and formed a cistern of lime and mortar ten yez by ten. On the four sides of the fountain a fine level platform for resting was constructed on a very neat plan. At the time when the arghwân flowers begin to blow, I do not know of any place in the world to be compared with it. The yellow arghwân is here very abundant, and the yellow arghwân blossom mingles with the red."

The Râm Bagh was the temporary resting-place of the body of Bâbar before it was taken to Kabul for interment in another of the gardens he loved so much. The old Mogul style of gardening is a lost art, and one misses in the Râm Bagh the stately rows of cypress, interspersed with flowering trees, the formal flower-beds glowing with colour like a living carpet, which were planted by Bâbar; but the terraces, the fountain, the water-channels, and the little stone water-shoots—cunningly carved so that the water breaks over them with a pleasant gurgling sound—which may have recalled to him the murmurings of his native mountain-streams—the old well from which the water of the Jumnâ is lifted into the channels, can still be seen, as well as the pavilions on the river-bank, now modernized with modern bad taste.

In later times the Râm Bagh was the garden-house of the Empress Nûr Mahall. It was kept up by all succeeding Governments, and it is said to have obtained its Hindu name from the Mahrattas in the eighteenth century.

THE ZUHARA BAGH.—Between the Chînî-kâ-Rauza and the Râm Bagh there is another great walled enclosure, which contained the garden-house of Zuhara, one of Bâbar's daughters, and is named after her the Zuhara, or Zohra Bagh. This formerly contained the largest garden-palace at Agra, and is said to have possessed no less than sixtv wells. A great well, just outside the enclosure, 220 feet in circumference, and of enormous depth, was filled up some years ago.

SIKANDRA

SIKANDRA, a village about five miles from Agra, and the burial-place of Akbar, is reached by two roads. The older one follows, to some extent, the alignment of the great military road to Lahore and Kashmir, planned by Bâbar and completed by his successors. A few of the *kos-minars*, pillars which marked off the *kos*—a distance of about two and a half miles—can still be seen along the road, or in the adjoining fields.

Numerous remains of archæological interest are passed on the way of the old road. First the Delhi gate of the old city walls. About a mile further, on the right-hand side, is a great walled enclosure, named after Ladli Begam, the sister of Abûl Fazl, Akbar's famous Prime Minister and biographer. It formerly contained her tomb, as well as that of Sheikh Mubarak, her father, and of Faizi, her eldest brother. Many years ago the whole enclosure was sold by Government. The purchasers, some wealthy Hindu merchants of Muttra, promptly pulled down the mausoleum, realized the materials, and built a pavilion on the site. In front of the great gateway was a splendid *baoli*, or well-house, the largest in the neighbourhood of Agra. This was filled up about five years ago.

Not far from Ladli Begam's garden is the Kandahâri Bagh, where the first wife of Shah Jahân, a daughter of Mozaffar Husein, who was the great-grandson of Shah Ismaîl Safvî, King of Persia, is buried.

About a mile further along the road, on the left-hand side, is a curious statue of a horse in red sandstone, which, tradition says, was put up by a nobleman whose favourite horse was killed at this spot; the syce who was killed at the same time has his tomb close by.

Nearly opposite to this is a large dried-up tank, called the Guru-ka-Tal, which, with the adjacent ruined buildings, are attributed to Sikandar Lodi, one of the Afghan predecessors of the Mogul Emperors, who has given his name to Sikandra.

Akbar's Tomb.

Akbar's tomb stands in the midst of a vast garden, enclosed by four high battlemented walls. In the centre of each wall is an imposing gateway seventy feet high. The principal one, on the west side, has an inscription in Persian, which states that the mausoleum was completed by the Emperor Jahângîr, in the seventh year of his reign, or

1612 A.D. It is elaborately ornamented with bold but rather disjointed inlaid patterns, which seem to show that the designers were unaccustomed to this method of decoration. Neither are the four minarets at the corners of the roof, which are said to have been broken by the Jâts, contrived with the usual skill of the Mogul architects. Above the gateway is the Nakkâr Khâna, an arcaded chamber witn a balcony, where at dawn and one watch after sunrise the drums and pipes sounded in honour of the dead.

The mausoleum was commenced by Akbar himself. It is different in plan from any other Mogul monument, being distinctly Hindu in character, and resembling the many-storied pavilions, used as assembly halls in Hindu and Buddhist monasteries, of which the Panch Mahall at Fatehpur Sîkrî is an example. The whole structure gives the impression of a noble but incompleted idea; both in its greatness and in its incompleteness, it is typical of Akbar and his work.

The original design was somewhat modified by Jahângîr. He has stated in his memoirs that on his first visit to the tomb after his accession he was dissatisfied with the work which had been done, and ordered certain parts of it to be rebuilt. Fergusson supposes that the original intention was to cover the tombstone and raised platform of the uppermost story with a domed canopy, and in this he is supported by a statement of William Finch, who visited the mausoleum when it was being built, that it was to be "inarched over with the most curious white and speckled marble, to be ceiled all within with pure sheet gold richly inwrought." Such a canopy is just what is required by æsthetic considerations to complete the curiously truncated appearance of the top story, and there is nothing in the structural design to make it impossible or improbable.

The approach to the interior of the mausoleum is through the central archway of the lower story, which opens into a vestibule richly ornamented with raised stucco work, and coloured in blue and gold, somewhat in the style of the Alhambra. A part of the decoration has been lately restored. An inclined passage, like the entrance to an Egyptian pyramid, leads down to a high vaulted chamber, dimly lighted from above, where a simple sarcophagus of white marble contains the mortal remains of the great Akbar. Whatever decoration there may have been on the walls is now covered with whitewash. The Emperor's armour, clothes and books, which were placed beside the tomb, are said to have been carried off by those insatiable marauders, the Jâts of Bharatpur.

Smaller chambers surrounding the central one,

Johnston and Hoffman, Photo.]

PLATE X.—MARBLE SARCOPHAGUS ON THE UPPER STORY OF AKBAR'S TOMB, SIKANDRA.

on the level of the platform, contain the tombs of two of Akbar's daughters and a son of the Emperor Shah Âlam. These also have suffered much from neglect and whitewash. The whole of the façade of the lower story was originally faced with red sandstone, or perhaps with fine stucco decorated in fresco. The present coat of common plaster is modern work, which, except as a protection for the brickwork, would have been better left undone.

The lower story is 320 feet square. Above this are three others, diminishing in size up to the highest, which is just half these dimensions. The roof of the topmost is surrounded by cloisters, the outer arches of which are filled with very fine marble tracery (Plate X.). In the centre, on a raised platform, is a solid block of pure white marble, delicately carved with flowers and sacred texts, representing the real tomb in the vault beneath. At the head is the inscripton, "Allah-o-Akbar" (God is Great), and at the foot, "Jalli Jalalohu" (Magnificent is His Glory). These sentences were the formula of Akbar's new religion, which he called "The Divine Faith." On the sides the ninety-nine attributes of God are carved in the Arabic character. The carved marble pedestal at the end of the tomb was a stand for a golden censer.

THE KANCH MAHALL.—Outside the enclosure of Akbar's tomb, a little to the east of the principal entrance, is a rare and remarkably fine example of Mogul domestic architecture. This is a two-storied building, known as the Kanch Mahall, and supposed to have been built by Jahângîr as a country seat. In its extremely elaborate ornamentation, inlaid stone and enamelled tiles have been most effectively combined with the carving. The repairs lately carried out under Lord Curzon's orders have been very carefully done, though it is easy to see the inferiority of the new work where the old carving had to be reproduced. Our fatuous policy of adopting European styles in all public buildings in India is bound to cause a deterioration in the native art handicrafts, for it closes the principal source from which they have sprung. Unless this policy is reversed, nothing will prevent the ultimate extinction of Indian art.

Sûraj-Bhan-kâ Bagh.—This is another two-storied building of about the same period, but not quite so fine in style, facing the Agra road, at a little distance from the Kanch Mahall.

Mariam Zâmâni's Tomb.—A short distance further on, in the direction of Muttra, is the building supposed to have been originally the garden house of Sikandar Lôdi, in which Mariam Zâmâni, one of Akbar's wives, is said to have been buried. It has been used for many years as a printing establishment for a Mission Orphanage.

OTHER BUILDINGS AND TOMBS AT OR NEAR AGRA

The tomb of Ferôz Khan, opposite to the third milestone on the Gwalior road, is an interesting building of Akbar's time richly carved and decorated with tile-work. Close by is the tomb of the Pahalwâri, where a celebrated wrestler of Shah Jahân's time is buried. There are a considerable number of buildings and numerous ruins in Agra, and round about, which possess only historical or archæological interest. In the town are the following:—

The Kâli Masjid, or Black Mosque, otherwise called the Kalan Masjid, or Grand Mosque, is of the early Akbar style. It was built by the father of Shah Jahân's first wife, the Kandahâri Begam. This is near to the Government dispensary.

In the Nai-ki-Mundi quarter is the mosque of Shah Alâ-ud-dîn Majzub, commonly known as Alawal Bilawal, a saint who lived at the time of Shêr Shah. He established a school of Muhammadan law, and founded a monastery besides the mosque. The accumulations round the mosque have reached up to the springing of the arches, and tradition accounts for this by the following story: A camel-driver in Shêr Shah's service stabled his beasts in the mosque, in spite of the protests of the saint. Thereupon the building began to sink into the ground, and did not cease descending until the camels and their driver were crushed to death.

The HAMMÂM, or Baths of Ali Verdi Khan, in Chipitolla Street, built in the time of Jahângîr. An inscription over the gateway gives the date, 1620 A.D. They cannot be compared in interest with the splendid "Hakîm's Baths," at Fatehpur Sîkrî.

The ROMAN CATHOLIC CEMETERY, in the quarter known as Padritollah, near the Law Courts, is one of the most ancient Christian cemeteries in India. The ground was granted to the mission by the Emperor Akbar. There are a number of Portuguese and Armenian tombs dating from early in the seventeenth century. The Tomb of Gerónimo Veroneo, the Italian to whom the design of the Taj has been wrongly attributed, has been lately discovered in this cemetery. It also contains the tomb of the notorious Walter Reinhardt, or Samru, as he was called, the founder of the principality of Sirdhana, whose history is given at p. 38. The Dutch General Hessing, who held Agra Fort for the Mahrattas in 1794, has a very florid mausoleum of red sandstone, more curious than beautiful, the design of which is in imitation of the Taj.

FATEHPUR SÎKRÎ

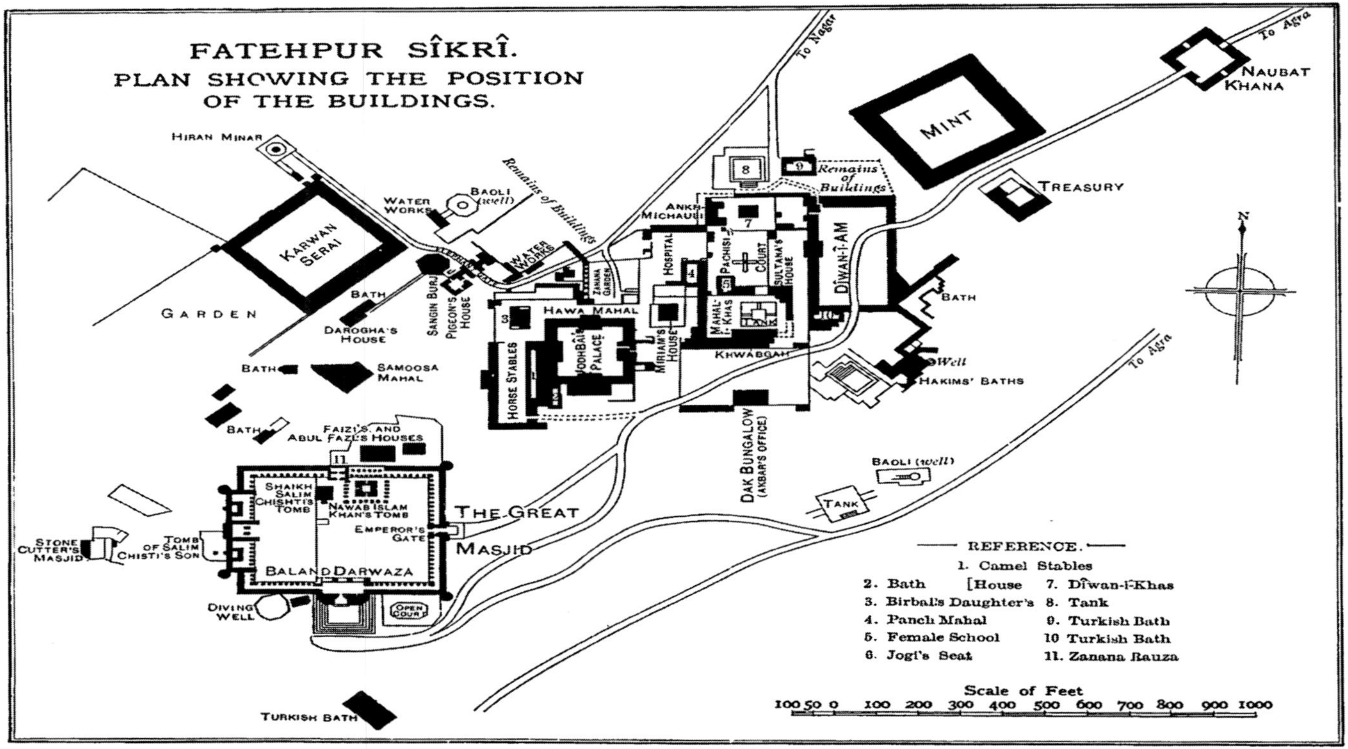

FATEHPUR SÎKRÎ.
PLAN SHOWING THE POSITION OF THE BUILDINGS.
HIRAN MINAR
KARWAN SERAI
GARDEN
WATER WORKS
BAOLI (well)
Remains of Buildings
WATER WORKS
SANGIN BURJ
PIGEON'S HOUSE
BATH
DAROGHA'S HOUSE
BATH
SAMOOSA MAHAL
BATH
FAIZI'S AND ABUL FAZL'S HOUSES
SHAIKH SALIM CHISHTI'S TOMB
NAWAB ISLAM KHAN'S TOMB
EMPEROR'S GATE
BALAND DARWAZA
THE GREAT MASJID
TOMB OF SALIM CHISTI'S SON
STONE CUTTER'S MASJID
DIVING WELL
OPEN COURT
TURKISH BATH
HAWA MAHAL
ZANANA GARDEN
HORSE STABLES
JODHBAI'S PALACE
MIRIAM'S HOUSE
HOSPITAL
ANKH-MICHAULI
PACHISI
COURT
SULTANA'S HOUSE
MAHAL-I-KHAS
TANK
KHWABGAH
DIWAN-I-AM
DAK BUNGALOW (AKBAR'S OFFICE)
To Nagar
Remains of Buildings
MINT
TREASURY
NAUBAT KHANA
To Agra
BATH
Well
HAKIMS' BATHS
BAOLI (well)
TANK
To Agra
N
REFERENCE.
1. Camel Stables
2. Bath
3. Birbal's Daughter's [House
4. Panch Mahal
5. Female School
6. Jogi's Seat
7. Dîwan-i-Khas
8. Tank
9. Turkish Bath
10 Turkish Bath
11. Zanana Rauza
Scale of Feet
100 50 0 100 200 300 400 500 600 700 800 900 1000

FATEHPUR SÎKRÎ

FATEHPUR SÎKRÎ is the famous deserted city, about twenty-three miles from Agra, built by Akbar. It was formerly merely a village, called Sîkrî, celebrated as the abode of Sheikh Salîm Chishti, a Muhammadan *pîr*, or saint. In 1564, Akbar, returning from a campaign, halted near the cave in which the saint lived. The twin children of his Rajput wife, Mariam Zâmâni, had recently died, and he was anxious for an heir. He consulted the holy man, who advised him to come and live at Sîkrî. The Emperor did so, and nine months afterwards Mariam, who was taken to Chishti's cell for her confinement, gave birth to a son, afterwards the Emperor Jahângîr. He was called Sultan Salîm in honour of the saint. Jahângîr, who describes all these circumstances in his memoirs, adds: "My revered father, regarding the village of Sîkrî, my birthplace, as fortunate to himself, made it his capital, and in the course of fourteen or fifteen years the hills and deserts, which abounded in beasts of prey, became converted into a magnificent city, comprising numerous gardens, elegant edifices and pavilions, and other places of great attraction and beauty. After the conquest of Gujerat, the village was named Fatehpur (the town of victory)."

The glory of Fatehpur Sîkrî was short-lived. Akbar held his court there for seventeen years, and then removed it to Agra; some say on account of the badness of the water supply, others that the saint, disturbed in his devotions by the bustle and gaieties of the great city, declared that either he or Akbar must go. "Then," replied the Emperor, "let it be your servant, I pray." The entire city was given up to the beasts of the surrounding jungle. Finch, who visited it in the early part of the next reign, describes it: "Ruin all; lying like a waste desert, and very dangerous to pass through in the night." This, however, was an exaggeration, for the principal buildings are still in a good state of preservation, probably owing to the remoteness of the place from any great highway or large town.

The city, which was some six miles in circuit, was surrounded on three sides by high battlemented walls, which had nine gateways. The fourth side was formed by a great artificial lake, now dry. The principal buildings are on the summit of the high ridge which runs throughout the length of the city.

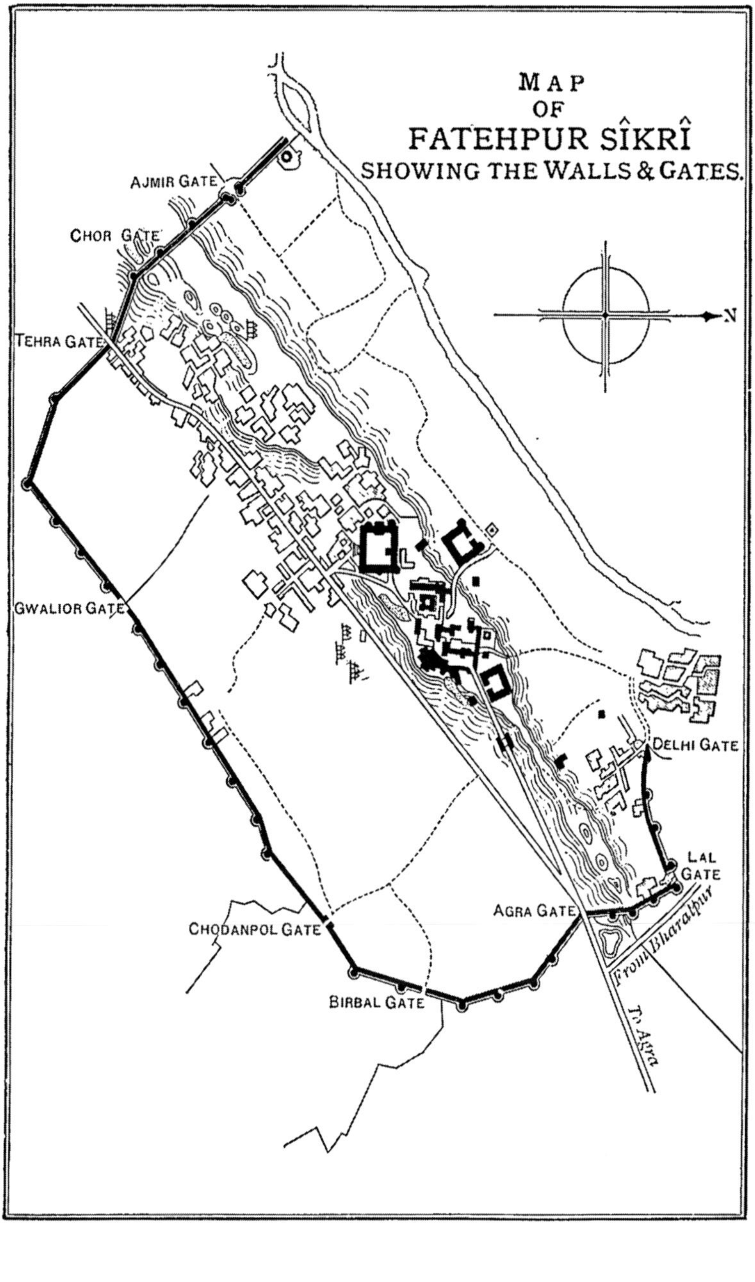
MAP
OF
FATEHPUR SÎKRÎ
SHOWING THE WALLS & GATES.
N
AJMIR GATE
CHOR GATE
TEHRA GATE
GWALIOR GATE
DELHI GATE
LAL
GATE
AGRA GATE
CHODANPOL GATE
BIRBAL GATE
From Bharatpur
To Agra

The Agra Gate.—The visitor usually enters by the Agra Gate, concerning which an amusing story is told. One night Akbar, attended by some of his ministers, was inspecting the ramparts near this gate, when he observed a highway robbery being committed close by the walls. Turning severely to those responsible for the peace of the city, he demanded why such an outrage was permitted in the very presence of the Emperor. "It is always darkest directly under the shadow of the lamp," was the courtly reply.

The Naubat Khâna.—Inside the gate the road passes, by the right, a large quadrangle surrounded by a ruined cloister, which was probably used for barracks. Beyond this the road was formerly lined on both sides by the houses of the bazar. It next passes through the inner gateway, called the *Naubat Khâna*, or Music House, where, as in all Mogul fortresses, the court musicians played to announce the Emperor's arrival or departure, and various state ceremonials.

The Mint.—Some distance beyond the Naubat Khâna, on the right, is a large building believed to have been the Imperial Mint. Rare specimens of gold, silver, and copper coins from the Fatehpur Mint are in the British Museum. The brick domes of this building are interesting, as they are probably the earliest examples in India of the use of radiating courses instead of horizontal layers in dome construction.

Opposite to the Mint is a smaller building known as the Treasury.

The Daftar Khâna.—Passing through the great quadrangle of the Dîwân-i-âm, the visitor arrives at the Daftar Khâna, or Record Chamber, now adapted for a travellers' rest-house. This was Akbar's office, and is immediately opposite to his own sanctum, the Kwâbgâh, and the principal buildings of the Imperial Palace. A staircase in the south-east room leads to the roof, from which a fine view of the city and surrounding country can be obtained. The principal buildings can be easily identified by help of the plan.

The Palace.—A door in the side of the quadrangle, opposite to the Daftar Khâna, leads into Akbar's palace, the Mahall-i-Khâs. The two-storied building on the left on entering contains Akbar's private apartments. The first room on the ground floor is panelled into numerous recesses for keeping books, documents, or valuables. There are some remains of painted decoration representing flowers, such as the tulip, poppy, and almond flower, executed with much vigour and technical skill. Behind this is a chamber which, according to Edmund Smith, was used by a Hindu priest attached to Akbar's court. It contains a stone platform raised on pillars, upon which he is said to have performed his devotions. It was more probably intended for Akbar's own gaddî, or throne. A door in the west wall leads into the cloisters, which formerly connected Akbar's apartments with the Daftar Khâna and with Jodh Bai's palace.

THE KWÂBGÂH, or sleeping apartment, is a small pavilion on the roof. Originally the walls were entirely covered by fresco paintings, but only a few fragments now remain. Unfortunately, these have been protected by a coat of varnish, which reduces them all to a dull monochrome. It is to be regretted that a more scientific method of preserving them was not adopted. They are all in the Persian style, and, except for the Chinese element which was very strong in Persian art of this period, there is no ground for Edmund Smith's supposition that Chinese artists were employed here.

On the side window over the eastern doorway is a painting of a winged figure, in front of a rock cave, supporting a new-born babe in its arms. In all probability it refers to the birth of Jahângîr in the cell of the Saint Salîm Chishti, which Akbar, no doubt, thought miraculous. Many archæologists make the great mistake of attributing every winged figure in these decorations to some Biblical story. Heavenly beings with wings, the inhabitants of Paradise, spirits of the air, or "angels," are very common in Persian and Indian painting, and are by no means a monopoly of European artists.

It is known that Akbar took a great interest in painting. Abûl Fazl, in the "Âîn-i-Akbarî," states that "His Majesty from the earliest youth has shown a great predilection for the art, and gives it every encouragement, as he looks upon it as a means both of study and amusement. Hence the art flourishes, and many painters have obtained great reputations. The works of all painters are weekly laid before his Majesty by the Daroghas and the clerks; he confers rewards according to the excellence of workmanship, or increases their monthly salaries. Much progress was made in the commodities required by painters, and the correct prices of such articles were carefully ascertained."

Akbar himself remarked, "Bigoted followers of the law are hostile to the art of painting, but their eyes now see the truth. There are many that hate painting, but such men I dislike. It appears to me as if a painter had a peculiar means of recognizing God; for a painter, in sketching anything that has life and in drawing its limbs, must feel that he cannot bestow personality upon his work, and is thus forced to think of God, the giver of life, and will thus increase his knowledge." The enlightened court of Akbar was evidently a paradise for artists.

Johnston and Hoffman, Photo.]

PLATE XI.—INTERIOR OF THE DÎWÂN-I-KHÂS, FATEHPUR SÎKRÎ.

Opposite to Akbar's apartments is a large square tank with a platform in the centre, approached by four narrow stone paths. The tank was filled from the waterworks near the Elephant Gate, and the water was kept constantly fresh by an overflow channel connecting with the tank at the back of the Dîwân-i-Khâs.

THE TURKISH SULTÂNA'S HOUSE.—In the north east angle of the Mahall-i-Khâs quadrangle is a small, picturesque building, one of the gems of Fatehpur, called the Turkish Sultâna's House. It contains only a single apartment, surrounded by a verandah, but in the carving of every surface within and without there is a wealth of invention and decorative skill rarely achieved even by the Mogul artists. The dado panels are especially remarkable for the charming conventionalized rendering of trees, flowers, birds, and animals. They have suffered much from the hands of some of Aurangzîb's fanatical followers, and all the representations of animate nature have been mutilated. The carving was intended as a groundwork for painting and gilding which were never added, for the Fatehpur Palace was abandoned even before it was finished. Nothing is known with certainty of the lady who inhabited this delightful bower, but she must have been one of Akbar's favourites. A covered passage connected the house with the

Kwâbgâh, and also with another block of buildings of no special interest, known as the Girls' School.

A staircase from the south verandah leads down to some interesting baths outside the south-west corner of the Dîwân-i-âm quadrangle, which were probably for the use of the Turkish Sultâna. They are worth seeing, though not so fine as the so-called Hakîm's Baths. The latter, which are situated just opposite to these baths, on the steep slope of the ridge, are the finest of their kind existing in India. They form an extensive hydropathic establishment, decorated in the most excellent taste with polished plaster and *sgraffito*, or cut-plaster work. Undoubtedly they were used by Akbar himself, and they derive their present name from their close proximity to the quarters occupied by the Hakîms, or doctors.

Pachîsî Board.—In the northern half of the great palace quadrangle is a *pachîsî* board, cut on the pavement, similar to the one in the Samman Burj in the Agra Fort. Here Akbar and the ladies of the Court would amuse themselves by playing the game with slave girls as living pieces. The dice were thrown on the small platform in the centre of the board.

The Dîwân-i-Khâs.—Further towards the north, immediately opposite to the Kwâbgâh, is a square detached building, a fine example of the dignified style of the period, for it owes none of its effects to imposing dimensions, but only to the skill with which the architect has treated a difficult subject. This is the Dîwân-i-Khâs, or Hall of Private Audience. On the outside it would appear to be a two-storied building, but on entering it is seen to contain only a single vaulted chamber, surrounded half-way up by a gallery. A magnificent carved column, with a gigantic bracket capital (Plate XI.), standing alone in the centre of the chamber, supports four branches or railed passages, which meet this gallery at the four corners. This most original construction, a Hindu symbol for the mystic "Pillar of the Universe,"[1] carried Akbar's throne, which was placed immediately over the great column. The ministers attended at the four corners of the gallery; the great nobles and others admitted to the audience thronged the floor beneath. The gallery is approached by two staircases, in the thickness of the walls, which also lead up to the roof.[2]

[1] See "Ideals of Indian Art," pp. 73–4.

[2] It is known that in 1575 Akbar completed a great building at Fatehpur, called the Ibadat Khâna, or hall in which the learned men of all religions assembled for discussion. It was described as containing four halls, the western for the Sayyids, or descendants of the Prophet; the southern for learned men who had studied or acquired knowledge; the northern for those famed for inspired wisdom; the eastern hall was reserved for the nobles and state officers. Thousands of people from all quarters of the world assembled in the courtyard. The Emperor attended every Friday night and on holy festivals, moving from one to the other of the guests and conversing with them. Keene, in his "Handbook to

The Ânkh-Michaulî.—Close by the Dîwân-i-Khâs, on the west side, is a building which the native guides, always ready to amuse the innocent tourists, describe as the Ânkh-Michaulî, or "Blind-man's Buff House." There is a legend that Akbar here played hide-and-seek with the ladies of the zanana. The same story is told about a set of apartments in the Jahângîrî Mahall in the Agra Fort, but the only ground for it seems to be that the arrangement of the rooms might lend itself to such diversions. It most probably contained strong-rooms for the safe custody of valuables, either state archives or jewels.

The Yogi's Seat.—At the corner of the Ânkh-Michaulî is a square platform covered by a domed canopy. The great carved brackets which support the architraves are very characteristic of Jaina temple construction. This was the seat of one of the Yogis, or Hindu fakirs, who enjoyed the Emperor's favour. Akbar devoted much attention to the occult powers claimed by these men. He

Agra," suggests that possibly the Dîwân-i-khâs may be the building thus described (taking the word *aiwan*, or hall, to mean a side gallery), as no other building at all answering to the description now remains at Fatehpur. This supposition is highly improbable, if only for the reason given by Edmund Smith, namely, that an assembly of this kind would not take place within the precincts of the palace. The description given by Abûl Fazl and Badâyûni clearly indicates a building like the Dîwân-i-âm, enclosing a great quadrangle.

even practised alchemy and showed in public some of the gold made by him.

THE HOSPITAL.—Adjoining the Ânkh-Michaulî are the remains of a long, low building, which was the hospital; a few of the wards still remain. Possibly this was arranged on the model of the hospital which Akbar allowed the Jesuit Fathers to build in the city. He also permitted them to construct a small chapel. The records of the missionaries tell us that Akbar once came there alone, removed his turban and offered prayers, first kneeling in the Christian manner, then prostrating himself according to the Muhammadan custom, and, finally, after the ritual of the Hindus. One of the Christian congregation having died about this time, he granted permission for the funeral procession to pass through the streets of Fatehpur with all the ceremonies of the Catholic faith. Many of the inhabitants, both Hindus and Muhammadans, attended the funeral. Akbar was never persuaded to become a convert to Christianity, nor does there appear to be any ground for the belief that one of his wives was a Christian.

THE DÎWÂN-I-ÂM.—The west side of the Dîwân-i-âm (Hall of Public Audience) and its cloisters coincide for the whole length with the east of the palace quadrangle. The description already given of the Dîwân-i-âm at Agra will explain the functions for which this building was intended. The throne, or judgment seat, of Akbar was placed between two pierced stone screens in the verandah in front of the hall.

THE PANCH MAHALL.—This curious five-storied pavilicn is nearly opposite to the Dîwân-i-âm. It is approached by a staircase from the Mahal-i-khâs. Each story was originally enclosed by pierced stone screens; this, and the fact that the whole building overlooked the palace zanana, make it tolerably certain that it could only have been used as a promenade by Akbar and the ladies of the Court. The ground-floor, which was divided into cubicles by screens between the columns, may, as Keene suggests, have been intended for the royal children and their attendants. The building is chiefly remarkable for the invention and taste shown in the varied designs of the columns, in which the principal styles of Northern India, Hindu, and Saracenic, are indiscriminately combined.

MIRIAM'S KÔTHÎ.—Another doorway in the west side of the palace quadrangle leads to Miriam's House, a very elegant two-storied building showing marked Hindu feeling in the design. The Râma incarnation of Vishnu appears on one of the carved brackets of the verandah. It seems to have derived its name from Akbar's Hindu wife, Mariam Zâmâni, the mother of Jahângîr. Her name literally means "Mary of the age," a common designation used by Muhammadan women in honour of the Mother of Jesus. This has led to the fable that the house was occupied by a Christian wife of Akbar. The whole building was originally covered with fresco paintings and gilding, and was hence called the Sunahrâ Makân, or "Golden House." The frescoes are supposed to illustrate Firdousi's great epic, the Shahnâma, or history of the Kings of Persia. As in the Kwâbgâh, the fragments which remain have been covered with varnish as a preservative, which has had the effect of destroying all the charm of colour they once possessed; and will eventually, when the varnish turns brown with age, obliterate them altogether. The paintings are all in the style of the Persian artists who were employed by Akbar to illustrate his books and to paint the portraits of his Court. Over the doorway in the north-west angle of the building is a painting which the guides, perhaps misled by the suggestion of some uninformed traveller, point out as "the Annunciation."

There would be nothing *primâ facie* improbable that Akbar should have caused some events of Biblical history to be painted on the walls of his palaces; but, on the other hand, there is nothing whatever to connect this fresco with the Annunciation. The winged figures here represented are of the type commonly found in paintings of stories from the Persian mythology.

Perhaps the most interesting of all the paintings is a portrait in a panel in one of the rooms. One would like to know whether this was the lady of the house; but there seems to be no tradition connected with it.

Judging from the style of the frescoes, it would seem probable that this was not the residence of Mariam Zâmâni, but of one of Akbar's first two wives, whose connections were mostly with Persia.

Jodh Bai's Palace.

Though "Miriam's House" is generally regarded as the abode of Mariam Zâmâni, there is a great deal to support the view that the spacious palace known as Jodh Bai's Mahall, or Jahângîrî Mahall, was really her residence. It is undoubtedly one of the oldest buildings in Fatehpur.

We know that Akbar went there on Mariam's account; and, after Jahângîr's birth, Akbar's first care would be to build a palace for the mother and her child, his long-wished-for heir. Mariam was a Hindu, and this palace in all its construction and nearly all its ornamentation belongs to the Hindu

PLAN OF
JODH BAI'S PALACE

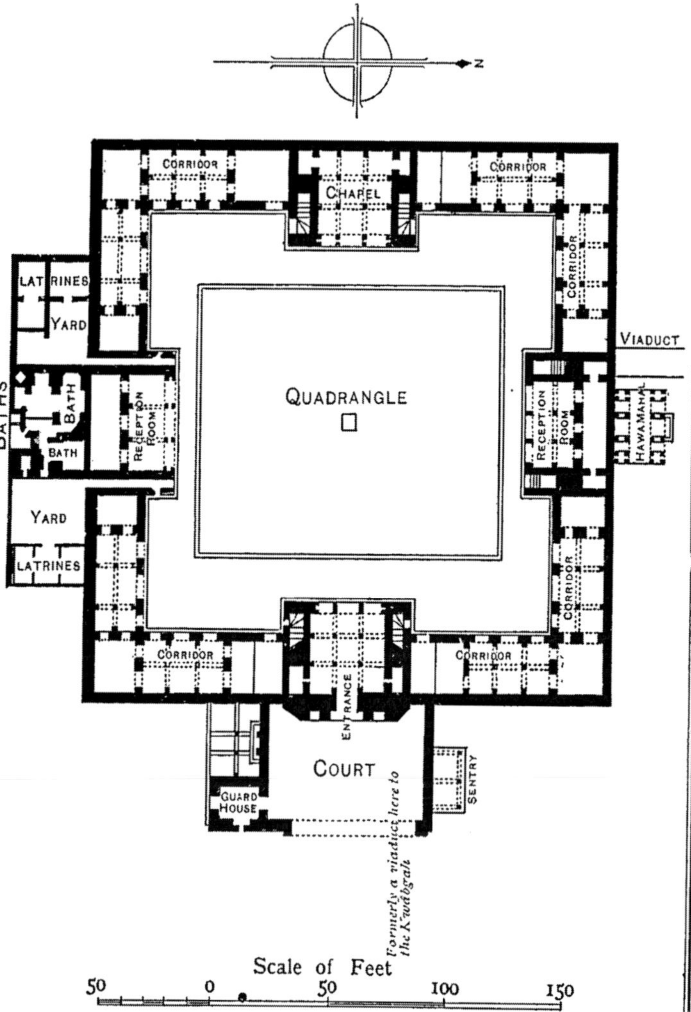

styles of Mariam's native country, Rajputâna. It even contains a Hindu temple.[1] It is also the most important of all the palaces, and Mariam, as mother of the heir-apparent, would take precedence of all the other wives.

On the left of the entrance is a small guardhouse. A simple but finely proportioned gateway leads through a vestibule into the inner quadrangle. The style of the whole palace is much less ornate than the other zanana buildings, but it is always dignified and in excellent taste. It must be remembered that the severity of the architectural design was relieved by bright colouring and rich purdahs, which were used to secure privacy for the ladies of the zanana and to diminish the glare of the sunlight.

Archæologically its construction and ornamentation are very interesting. Many of the details are of the same type as the mixed Hindu and Saracenic style, which was being developed about

Keene suggests that Akbar's first wife and cousin, Sultana Raqia Begam, lived here, but she was a Muhammadan. It is quite possible that the name of Jodh Bai (Princess of Jodhpur) really refers to Mariam, and not to Jahângîr's Rajput wife (the daughter of the Raja of Jodhpur), as is commonly supposed. Mariam's family resided in the province of Ajmir, which adjoins Jodhpur. She might have been known as the Princess of Jodhpur. In any case, it is easy to see how a confusion might have arisen between Jahângîr's mother and his wife, both Hindus and Rajputs.

the same period in Gujerat. The arrangements of the palace are shown in the annexed plan. One of the most interesting features is the Hawâ Mahall, a pavilion projecting from the north side, enclosed by pierced stone screens. Here the ladies could enjoy the cool breezes and the view of the lake with the distant hills beyond, without being exposed to the vulgar gaze. The palace was formerly connected with Akbar's private apartments by a covered way, supported on pillars, near the entrance. This was removed some years ago. Another private passage led from the Hawâ Mahall to the zanana garden opposite, and, probably, from thence right down to the tower known as the Hiran Minâr.

Rajah Birbal's House, or Birbal's Daughter's House.

Rajah Birbal was a Brahman minstrel, who came to Akbar's court in the beginning of his reign, and by his wit and abilities gained the Emperor's favour. He was first created Hindu Poet Laureate; from that dignity he was raised to the rank of Rajah, and became one of Akbar's most intimate friends and advisers. Birbal was one of those who subscribed to Akbar's new religion, "The Divine Faith." When he perished in an unfortunate

Johnston and Hoffman, Photo.]

PLATE XII.—RAJAH BIRBAL'S DAUGHTER'S HOUSE, FATEHPUR SÎKRÎ.

expedition against some unruly Afghan tribes, Akbar's grief was for a long time inconsolable.

The house which is named after him was originally enclosed within the precincts of the imperial zanana, and a covered way connected it with Jodh Bai's palace. It is one of the most richly decorated of all the adjacent buildings, and next to Jodh Bai's palace, the largest of the imperial residences. As in so many other instances, the vague local tradition which assigns this palace to Rajah Birbal seems to be at fault. Abûl Fazl, that most careful and precise biographer, records that Akbar ordered a palace to be built for the Rajah, and that when it was finished in the twenty-seventh year of his reign (1582) the Emperor honoured it with his presence. An inscription discovered by Edmund Smith upon the capital of a pilaster in the west façade of the building, states that it was erected in Samvat 1629 (A.D. 1572), ten years before this date, and three years after the commencement of the city.

Though the Rajah was one of Akbar's most trusted friends, his palace would hardly be placed within the enclosure of the Emperor's own zanana and connected with it; nor is it likely that Akbar would provide Birbal with a residence so incomparably more magnificent than those he gave to his other two intimate friends, Abûl Fazl and Faizi, by the side of the great mosque.

All the probabilities are that this was one of the imperial palaces occupied by Akbar's wives, which were the first buildings erected at Fatehpur. Fergusson's assumption that Birbal's daughter was one of Akbar's wives would explain everything; but the fact that Abûl Fazl makes no mention of such a daughter, is very good evidence that Akbar was not connected with Birbal by marriage.

The house is a two-storied building, splendidly ornamented with carving, both inside and out. From the construction, it would appear that Hindus were the architects; but the decoration, from which it is easy to discover the taste of the occupants, is nearly all Arabian or Persian in style, and conveys no suggestion that the palace was built for a Hindu rajah or his daughter. Though on a much smaller scale, it is of the same type as Akbar's splendid palace in the Agra Fort, and was evidently intended for one of the highest rank in the imperial zanana.[1]

[1] Birbal's house is now used as a travellers' rest-house for high officials and "distinguished" visitors; which is not only very inconvenient for the undistinguished who may wish to see it, but involves alterations which should never be permitted in buildings of such unique artistic and archæological interest. Neither the Daftar Khana nor this building should be devoted to such purposes, merely to avoid the paltry expense of providing proper dak bungalows.

The Hâthî Pôl and Adjoining Buildings.

Close under Birbal's house is the main road leading down to the great lake—now drained, the embankment of which formed the north-west boundary of the city. It passes through the gateway called the Hâthî Pôl, or Elephant Gate, from the two great stone elephants, mutilated by Aurangzîb, standing on either side of the outer archway. On the left of the gateway are two buildings, the so-called Pigeon's House, probably intended for a magazine; and the Sangin Burj, a great bastion supposed to be part of the fortifications begun by Akbar and left unfinished, owing to the objections of Sheikh Salîm Chishti. A little beyond this, on the right, are the remains of the waterworks which supplied the whole city. Opposite to these is the great traveller's rest-house, or Karwân-serai, in a very ruined state.

The furthest of this block of buildings is a curious tower called the Hiran Minâr, or Deer Tower, 72 feet in height, ornamented with stone imitations of elephant tusks. According to tradition, it was built by Akbar in memory of a favourite elephant, and used by him as a shooting tower; the plain on the margin of the lake being the haunt of antelope and other game.

The splendid stretch of water, six miles long and two in breadth, induced many of the princes and nobles to build pavilions and garden houses on this side of the city. This was the place for great tournaments and festivities, and in the palmy days of Fatehpur all the chivalry of the Mogul Court must have made a brave show here. The Hiran Minâr was connected with the zanana by a covered way, so that the ladies might assist at these spectacles and enjoy the cool breezes from the lake.

The Jâm'i Masjid, or Cathedral Mosque.

The great mosque of Fatehpur is worthy of its founder's lofty ideals and nobility of soul. It is one of the most magnificent of all Akbar's buildings; the historic associations connected with it combine with its architectural splendour to make it one of the most impressive of its kind in the world. It is said to be copied from one at Mecca; but this cannot be altogether true, because, though the plan and general design follow Muhammadan precedent, many of the details show Akbar's Hindu proclivities

Within the great mosque, Akbar frequently held religious discussions with the learned doctors of Islam; and here, also, after the chief Mullahs had signed the famous document which declared Akbar to be Head of the Church, the Emperor mounted the pulpit, and stood before the congregation as the expounder of "the Divine Faith." He commenced to read a *Khutbah*, or litany, which Faizi, Abûl Fazl's brother, had composed for the occasion—

> "The Lord, who gave to us dominion,
> Wisdom, and heart and strength,
> Who guided us in truth and right,
> And cleansed our mind from all but right,
> None can describe His power or state,
> Allahú Akbar—God is great."

But before he could finish three lines of it, the sense of the tremendous responsibility he had undertaken overpowered him. He descended the pulpit trembling with emotion, and left the Imam of the mosque to continue the service.

There are two entrances, approached by broad flights of steps. The one on the east side is the Emperor's Gate, by which Akbar entered the mosque from the palace, and the other, the majestic Buland Darwâza, or High Gate, which towers above everything on the south side, and even dwarfs the mosque itself with its giant proportions. The latter gate, however, was not a part of the original design, but was added many years after the completion of the mosque, to celebrate Akbar's victorious campaign in the Deccan.

The mosque itself was built in honour of the

Saint of Fatehpur, Sheikh Salîm Chishti, whose tomb, enclosed in a shrine of white marble, carved with the delicacy of ivory-work, glitters like silver on the right of the quadrangle. Barren women, both Hindu and Muhammadan, tie bits of string or shreds of cloth to the marble trellis-work as tokens that if blessed with a son they will present an offering to the shrine. Close by is a plainer, but much larger mausoleum, for his grandson, Nawab Islam Khan, who was made Governor of Bengal by Jahângîr. This also contains the remains of many other of the Sheikh's male descendants. A separate vault, called the Zanana Rauza, for the women of his family, is formed by enclosing a portion of the adjoining cloisters.

The mosque proper contains three chapels, crowned by domes. The principal one, in the centre, is screened by the façade of the entrance, the doorway being recessed, in the usual style of Saracenic buildings, in a great porch or semi-dome. An inscription over the main archway gives the date of the completion of the mosque as A.D. 157 . The chapels are connected with each other by noble colonnades of a decidedly Hindu character. The Saracenic arches combine most happily with the Hindu construction, and the view down the "long-drawn aisles" is singularly impressive. Much of the charm of the interior is due to the quiet reserve

PLATE XIII.—THE BULAND DARWÂZA, FATEHPUR SÎKRÎ.

and dignity of the decoration, which is nearly all in the style of Arabian mosques, and may account for the statement on the central arch, that "this mosque is a duplicate of the Holy Place" (at Mecca).[1]

At each end of the mosque there is a set of five rooms for the mullahs who conducted the service; above them are galleries for the ladies of the zanana. Spacious cloisters surround three sides of the quadrangle; these are divided into numerous cells for the *maulvis* and their pupils.

The triumphal gateway, called the Buland Darwâza (Plate XIII.), is really a building in itself. It must be seen from the outside of the quadrangle, for, magnificent as it is there, it certainly does not harmonize with the mosque viewed from the quadrangle. This mighty portal, 176 feet in height from the roadway, is a landmark for miles around. From the top of it the Taj, twenty-five miles away, and the distant Fort of Bharatpur are visible.

There are three doors recessed in the immense alcove on the front of the gate. One is the horseshoe door, so called from the numerous votive offerings of owners of sick horses, donkeys, and

[1] It says much for Akbar's wonderful artistic intuition, that even when he used a foreign building for a model the imitation was never a mechanical copy, but an artistic adaptation designed to make the best use of local opportunities and requirements.

bullocks, which were nailed on in the hope of obtaining the favour of the saint. The doorway on the right of this has the following inscription carved over it in Arabic:—

"His Majesty, King of kings, Heaven of the Court, Shadow of God, Jalâl-ud-dîn Muhammad Akbar, Emperor. He conquered the kingdom of the South and Dandes, which was formerly called Khandes, in the 46th Divine year [*i.e.* of his reign] corresponding to the Hijira year, 1010 [A.D. 1602]. Having reached Fatehpur, he proceeded to Agra. Said Jesus, on whom be peace! The world is a bridge, pass over it, but build no house there. He who hopeth for an hour, may hope for eternity; the world is but an hour, spend it in devotion; the rest is worth nothing."

Over the left doorway is the following:—

"He that standeth up in prayer, and his heart is not in it, does not draw nigh to God, but remaineth far from Him. Thy best possession is what thou givest in the name of God; thy best traffic is selling this world for the next."

Akbar himself died four years after this great sermon in stone was written.

The Stone-Cutters' Mosque.

At the back of the great mosque is a graveyard containing the tomb of an infant son of Sheikh

Salîm. The legend concerning him is, that at the age of six months he addressed his father, telling him that all of Akbar's children must die in infancy, unless some child died for them. He therefore had resolved to sacrifice himself for the Emperor's sake, and immediately after this miraculous speech he died. Jahângîr was born nine months afterwards. Sceptics have suggested that he was really a son of the Sheikh, substituted for a still-born child of Mariam Zâmâni.

Some distance beyond this tomb there is a small mosque, built in honour of the saint by the quarrymen of Fatehpur, before he had attracted the notice of the great Emperor. It is called the Stone-Cutters' Mosque, and is supposed to have been erected on the site of the cave where he lived the life of a hermit. It is an unpretending little building; the brackets which support the cornice are the only noticeable architectural features. They are direct imitations of wooden construction, and are copied, with greater elaboration of carving, in the marble shrine inside the Jâm'i Masjid. The cell where the saint is said to have lived is on the right-hand corner of the mosque.

The birthplace of Jahângîr is pointed out in a dilapidated palace not far from this mosque. It is occupied by a lineal descendant of Salîm Chishti, and is only rarely shown to visitors.

The Houses of Abûl Fazl and Faizi.

The houses where these two famous brothers, the friends of Akbar, lived, are close under the north wall of the great mosque. Their father, Sheikh Mubarak, was one of the most learned men of the age, and the sons were as distinguished as the father. Faizi was the Persian Poet Laureate, and tutor to the Royal Princes. He was also employed on many diplomatic missions. Abûl Fazl was the author of the celebrated "Akbar-nâma," a history of the Mogul Emperors down to the forty-seventh year of Akbar's reign. He was for a long time Akbar's Prime Minister; he took a prominent part in the religious discussions inaugurated by the Emperor, and often discomfited the orthodox followers of Islam with his arguments. Sheikh Mubarak drew up the famous document declaring Akbar to be the Head of the Church, and both his sons subscribed to it. Abûl Fazl declares that the document "was productive of excellent results: (1) The Court became the resort of the learned men and sages of all creeds and nationalities; (2) Peace was given to all, and perfect tolerance prevailed; (3) the disinterested motives of the Emperor, whose labours were directed to a search after truth, were rendered clear, and the pretenders to learning and scholarship were put to shame."

Notwithstanding his high character and generous disposition, Abûl Fazl had many enemies at Court. He was at last assassinated at the instigation of Jahângîr, who believed him to be responsible for a misunderstanding between himself and his father.

There is nothing architecturally interesting about the two houses, which have been for some time used as a Zillah school.

Bharatpur and Other Places in the Vicinity of Agra.

There are some other places of considerable interest easily accessible from Agra, but it would be beyond the scope of this book to describe them in detail.

BHARATPUR.—This place, which has been often alluded to, is the capital of a native state of that name, founded by the Jâts under Sûraj Mall about 1750. The origin of the Jât race is obscure, but probably they are of Scythiar descent. Some authorities have put forward a theory that the gypsies of Europe and the Jâts are of the same race.

They form a large proportion of the population of North-Western India. Their religion varies with the locality, but the Jâts who occupied Agra under Sûraj Mall were Hindus.

In 1809, the fort at Bharatpur resisted for six weeks a siege by General, afterwards Lord Lake, who withdrew, after four desperate assaults.

The Palace of Sûraj Mall is at Dîg, twenty-one miles by road from Bharatpur. It was commenced about 1725, and is the finest and most original of the Indian palaces of that period. The Jât chief carried off to it a great deal of the loot from the Agra Fort.

GOVARDHAN.—The tombs of Sûraj Mall and his two Rânis are at Govardhan, a very picturesque place about eight miles from Dîg. There are also a number of very interesting tombs and buildings of later date. Fergusson[1] says of one of these, which was in course of construction when he was there in 1839, that he acquired from its native architect more knowledge of the secrets of art as practised in the Middle Ages than he had learnt from all the books he had read. The same living architectural art is practised all over Rajputana at the present day. The preference we show for the incomparably inferior art of the mongrel eclectic styles we have imported into India, is only a proof

[1] "History of Indian and Eastern Architecture."

that there is something wanting in the superior civilization and culture which we believe ourselves to possess.

There is also at Govardhan a very fine Hindu temple, dating from the time of Akbar.

A great fair is held here every year about the end of October, or beginning of November, on the occasion of the Hindu Dîwâli, or Feast of Lamps, one of the most beautiful and impressive of all the Hindu festivals.

MUTTRA, the Mathora of the Greeks, about fourteen miles from Govardhan, and within easy reach of Agra by rail, is one of the most sacred places of the Hindus, from being the reputed birthplace of Krishna. It is a great centre for the worship of Vishnu, as Benares is for that of Siva.

BRINDÂBAN, or BINDRÂBAN, which is a very short distance further by rail, possesses an old Hindu temple, dedicated to Govind Deva, or Vishnu, of the same period as the other at Govardhan, and built by the same person, Rajah Man Singh of Amber, an ancestor of the present Maharajah of Jaipur. Fergusson describes it as one of the most interesting and elegant temples in India.

There is also a great Vishnu temple of the last century, in the Dravidian style of Southern India, built by a Hindu millionaire merchant. Krishna's childhood and early youth were passed in the vicinity of Brindâban, and on that account it is held especially sacred by the followers of the Vaishnavite sect of Hinduism, who flock there in thousands on the anniversary of Krishna's birth, in the month of Bhadon (August—September).

APPENDIX

I. The Designers of the Taj.

SINCE this handbook was first published in 1904, there has been a lively discussion on the question of the validity of the long accepted European tradition that the Taj was designed by an Italian architect. It seems desirable, therefore, to restate the grounds in which I believe an impartial historian will refuse to accept the single uncorroborated statement of a Spanish Augustinian Friar, Father Manrique, who visited Agra in 1640, when the Taj was under construction, and recorded in his journal the following story from information given him by the Jesuit Fathers at Agra and Lahore :—

"The architect was a Venetian, named Geronimo Veroneo, who came to India with the ships of the Portuguese and died at Lahore a little before my arrival . . . Of him a report was current that the Padsha, having sent for him and made known to him the desire he felt to build there [at Agra] a sumptuous and grandiose monument to his defunct consort, the architect Veroneo obeyed, and in a few days produced various models of very fine architecture showing all the skill of his art; also that, having contented his Majesty in this, he dissatisfied him according to his barbarous and arrogant pride—by the modesty of his estimates; further that, growing angry, he ordered him to spend three krors, and to let him know when they were spent."

Now, if Father Manrique and his fellow priests had any special interest in or knowledge of architectural questions and we could believe that they had taken pains to ascertain the facts regarding this Italian adventurer's supposed connection with the Taj, the evidence on this side of the case might seem to be strong. But, both in the seventeenth century and in the present day, travellers' notes in foreign lands on matters not directly concerned with the object of their journey can rarely, when taken by themselves, be accepted as history without further evidence. The evidence for the European design of the Taj rests on this casual statement of Father Manrique alone —no other writer corroborates it. Tavernier, who saw both the commencement and completion of the Taj, neither mentions Veroneo nor gives any suggestion that the building was in any way the work of a European. Bernier in his description of the Taj makes it clearly understood that he looked upon it as a purely Oriental conception, for he naïvely confesses that he would not have ventured to express his great admiration for it if Tavernier, his companion, had not approved his taste; he feared that it might have been corrupted by his long residence in the Indies, and it was quite a relief to his mind to hear Tavernier say that he had seen nothing in Europe so bold and majestic. Bernier makes the important statement that no Christian was allowed to enter the Mausoleum lest its sanctity be profaned. Thévenot, who saw the Taj in 1666, was likewise silent on the subject of Veroneo, and declared that "this superb monument is sufficient to show that Indians are not ignorant of architecture, and though the style may appear curious to Europeans, it is in good taste, and though it is different from Greek or other ancient art, one can only say it is very fine."

The statements of these three trustworthy travellers who expressed a lively interest in the Taj not only furnish no corroboration of Father Manrique's report, but give strong negative evidence against its accuracy. On the same side are the inherent improbabilities that Shah Jahân should have placed a European in the position claimed for Veroneo. At the time the Taj was built the position of the Franks, as

Europeans were called, at the Mogul court was very different to what it was in the reigns of Akbar and Jahangîr. They were mostly employed in the artillery, and Bernier tells us that in his time they were admitted with difficulty into the service ; and that whereas formerly, when the Moguls were little skilled in the management of artillery, they received as much as 200 rupees a month, their pay was now limited to 32 rupees. The Jesuits, who had enjoyed high favour under the two former Emperors, were bitterly persecuted by Shah Jahân. He deprived them of their pension, destroyed the church at Lahore and a greater part of that at Agra, demolishing a steeple which contained a clock heard in every part of the city. Only a short time before her death, Mumtâz Mahall, who was a relentless enemy of the Christians, had instigated Shah Jahân to attack the Portuguese settlement at Hûghli. The defenders, after a desperate resistance, were overwhelmed, and 2000 of them, including women and children, who took refuge on a warship, perished with the crew as the captain blew up the vessel rather than surrender. Five hundred prisoners, among them some Jesuit priests, were sent to Agra. The Empress, with threats of torture, endeavoured to persuade the priests to renounce their religion. On their refusal they were thrown into prison, but some months afterwards they were released and deported to the main Portuguese settlement at Goa. It seems probable that Veroneo paid some of the ransom for these prisoners from his own purse, and this, rather than his supposed connection with the Taj, would account for the mention of his name by the Jesuit Fathers and for the removal of his body from Lahore, where he died, to Agra. The recently reported discovery of his tomb at the latter place, is of no value as evidence for or against his connection with the Taj.

Against Father Manrique's statement are also to be placed the detailed history of the building given by contemporary Indian writers, all of which agree that the chief designers were Ustâd Îsâ, from Shiraz or from *Rûm* (a term used loosely to designate Constantinople or any place in Asiatic Turkey) and his son Muhammad Sharîf. The Taj itself, by far the most important evidence in the case, lends no colour to the highly improbable suggestion that Shah Jahân, whose lifelong devotion to his wife was the strongest trait in his character, made one of the hated unbelievers the chief architect of her monument. The building shows hardly the smallest trace of the influence of the Italian Renaissance, which would certainly have made itself conspicuous if an Italian of the seventeenth century had been the chief designer. The evolution of the design from that of previous Mogul buildings can be clearly traced: the plan and general arrangement follow closely the design of Humâyûn's tomb, built by Akbar nearly a century earlier. The suggestion that Shah Jahân, surrounded by all the most accomplished architects of the East, might have engaged a European to design a building strictly according to Eastern ideals would only seem plausible to critics who do not understand the essential difference between modern architectural eclecticism and the practice of the seventeenth century. If the remarkable story regarding this obscure adventurer is true it must have been that his genius was so entirely permeated by the spirit of the East that he had ceased to think in a European way. In that case the question of his nationality has only an academic interest: the glory of the creation of the Taj would still belong to India.

The rejection of Father Manrique's statement need not imply that Veroneo had nothing to do with the Taj. He might have been one of the council of architects appointed by Shah Jahân to consider the design of the monument. He might even have had some share in the initial construction of the building when the design was approved. But this is very far from making him the chief architect of the Taj.

Another casual statement of Father Manrique, that a Frenchman, named Austin (or Augustin) de Bordeaux, was employed in "internal decorations" of the Taj, is the sole foundation for the Anglo-Indian supposition that the latter designed or superintended the magnificent inlaid decoration of the exterior and interior, technically known in Europe by the Italian name of "*pietra dura.*" It is highly probable that Austin was the goldsmith and jeweller, of very doubtful reputation, mentioned by Bernier as having been employed by Shah Jahân in making the famous Peacock Throne. Tavernier stated that Shah Jahân had intended to employ him in covering with silver the vault of a great gallery in the palace at Agra, so it is quite possible that he may have, as I suggest on p. 75, executed some of the gold and silver work inside the Taj, but on technical grounds it is difficult to understand why a French goldsmith and jeweller should be made responsible for inlaid stone work, similar in technique but totally different in design to Florentine *pietra dura.* The Florentine panels inserted at the back of the Throne Chamber in the Dîwân-i-âm at Delhi are most probably a good many years later in date than the Taj; but even if some specimens of the kind were shown to Shah Jahân and took his fancy, so that he ordered his craftsmen to use this kind of decoration, the only point of artistic importance is that the Taj decorations are more delicately beautiful and finer in taste than any Florentine *pietra dura* that was ever made.

The technique of *pietra dura* was probably practised by Indian craftsmen long before the time of Austin de Bordeaux. The Indian records show that the inlay workers of the Taj were not Persian, but mostly Hindus from Kanauj, which seems to show that similar technical methods had a long tradition behind them in India. After all *pietra dura* is only an adaptation to stone of methods of gold and silver inlay practised by Indian craftsmen from time immemorial. The designs of the Taj inlay were mostly adapted from Persian floral motifs, exactly similar to those on the illuminated borders of three Indian miniature paintings of Jahângîr's time now in the Calcutta Art Gallery. One of them bears the date 1624 A.D., or eight years before the Taj was commenced.

II. Hindu Influence in Mogul Architecture.

Bâbar's somewhat contemptuous description of the state of Hindustan, as he found it—its want of irrigation works and suitable buildings—might appear to justify the commonly accepted belief that the Moguls owed little to the Hindus, except as artisans, in their great building operations; and that the creative inspiration, both constructive and decorative, of Mogul architecture, was almost exclusively foreign to India. A careful study of history and analysis of Indian architecture will prove that this was very far from being the case. Bâbar was only describing the desolation produced in that part of India, with which he became acquainted, by the devastating armies of Islam, for several centuries before his time. During these centuries India had surrendered to her Muhammadan foes hundreds and thousands of her masons and master-builders, whose lives were spared in the general massacre which marked the path of the invaders, so that their skill might be utilized in adorning the great cities of Central and Western Asia. Bâbar's ancestor, Tîmûr, had used Indian as well as Arabian, Persian, and Chinese architects in building his mosques and palaces at Samarkand. The testimony of Muhammadan writers shows how great was their admiration for the architectural works of the Hindus. Alberuni, the Arabian historian who visited India in the eleventh century, was amazed at the skill of the Hindu builders, especially in the construction of bathing tanks, the absence of which Bâbar deplored. "In this," he wrote, "they have attained to a very high degree of art, so that our people (the Muslims), when they see them, wonder at them, and are unable to describe them, much less to construct anything like them."

Although Jahângîr and Shah Jahân undoubtedly imported architects and designers from Persia and Western Asia, it is necessary to remember how much the ancestors of these men had learnt from India; some of them might have been descendants of Indian captives taken by the armies of Islam. The Mogul buildings themselves testify how much these imported architects were indebted to their Hindu collaborators, for the Indian branches of the Saracenic style of architecture far surpass in richness of imagination and in constructive skill any of their contemporaries. Many of the most essential constructive and ornamental details of the Mogul style in its zenith are of Indian origin. The beautiful device of making the contours of a dome spring from the heart of a lotus flower, which gives both the Taj Mahall and the monuments of Bijapur their exquisite "sky-line," is a purely Indian conception. The original method of construction adopted in the colossal dome of Mahmud's monument at Bijapur, described by Fergusson as a wonder of constructive skill far surpassing any similar European building, is an ingenious adaptation of the Hindu system of temple roofing for balancing the weight of the Saracenic dome. The deep projecting bracketed cornices of the Mogul buildings are also adapted from a conspicuous feature in Hindu temple architecture.

On the whole, though the Moguls were the paymasters and retained the executive control, and though their customs and religious ritual dictated the general forms and arrangement of their buildings, it would appear that the artistic genius which inspired their design was more often Hindu than Muhammadan. In any case, it is entirely wrong to assume, as European writers have done, that the Indian builders were wholly tutored and artistically directed by the genius of their Mogul masters.

INDEX

ABÛL Fazl, murder of, 26, 133; history written by, 132; house of, 132
Agra, early history of, 3; Bâbar's connection with, 13; Akbar's connection with, 25; Jahângîr's connection with, 28; monuments of Shah Jahân's reign at, 32; history under later Mogul Emperors, 37; in the Mutiny, 39; Agra Fort, 40; Delhi Gate, 40; Darshan Darwâza, 45; Diwân-i-âm, 46; inner Mîna Bazar, 51; Chitor Gates, 52; Hindu Temple, 53; Machchî Bhawân, 53; supposed prison of Shah Jahân, 54; Najîna Masjid, 54; Dîwân-i-Khâs, 55; Jahângîr's throne, 56; the Baths, 57; Samman Burj, 57; Khâs Mahall, 59; Angûrî Bâgh, 61; Shîsh Mahall, 62; "Somnath" Gates, 62; Jahângîrî Mahall, 63; Salîmgarh, 67
Akbar, founded modern Agra, 3; life of, 18; administrative reforms, 21; religious belief, 22; connection with Agra, 25; death, 25; apartments in Agra Fort, 65; tomb of, 97; interest in painting taken by, 112
Akbarâbâd, 3
Alawal Bilawal, mosque of, 18, 102
Ali Verdi Khan, baths of, 29, 103
Angûrî Bagh, 59, 61

BÂBAR, life of, 4; memoirs, 7, 10; death, 11; connection with Agra, 13; gardens of, 14, 92; road to Kabul begun by, 15
Bairam Khan, 19, 20
Bernier, French traveller, 33, 47
Bharatpur, 133
Bindrâban, 135
Birbal, Rajah, house of, 122
Buland Darwâza, Fatehpur Sîkrî, 127, 129
Buland Khan, tower of, 29
Bordeaux, Austin de, 75 *and Appendix I.*
Brindâban, 135

CEMETERY, Roman Catholic, Agra, 103
Charnock, Job, 37
Chinghiz Khan, 4
Chînî-kâ-Rauza, 61
Chishti, Sheikh Salîm, 107; tomb of, 128
Chitor Gates, 52

DANSA Jât, house of, 43
Dârâ Shukoh, 30, 33
Darshan Darwâza, 42, 45
Dîg, palace of, 134
Dîn-i-ilâhi, 23, 24, 127
Dîwâli, feast of, 135
Dîwân-i-âm, Agra, 46
„ Fatehpur Sîkrî, 117
Dîwân-i-Khâs, Agra, 55
„ Fatehpur Sîkrî, 114

ELEPHANT Gate, Agra, 40, 41
" " Fatehpur Sîkrî, 125
Elephant statues, Agra, 40, 41
Emperor's Gate, Fatehpur Sîkrî, 127

FAIZI, 96
Fatehpur Sîkrî, battle of, 11; city of, 107; Agra Gate, 109; Naubat Khâna, 109; The Mint, 109; Daftar Khâna, or Record Chamber, 110; the Palace, 110; Kwâbgâh, 111; Turkish Sultana's house, 113; Hakîm's Baths, 114; pachîsî board, 114; Dîwân-i-Khâs, 114; Ânkh-Michaulî, 116; Yogi's Seat, 116; hospital, 117; Dîwân-i-âm, 117; Panch Mahall, 118; Miriam's Kôthî, 118; Rajah Birbal's house, 122; Hâthî Pôl, 125; Pigeon's House, 125; Sangin Burj, 125; Karwân-serai, 125; Hiran Minâr, 125; Jâm'i Masjid, 126; Buland Darwâza, 129; Stone-Cutters' Mosque, 130; houses of Abûl Fazl and Faizi, 132
Fazl, Abûl, 25, 132, 133
Feroz Khan, tomb of, 102
Firokhshiyar, 37

GOVARDHAN, 134
Guru-ka-Tal, 98

HÂTHÎ Pôl, Agra, 40, 41
" " Fatehpur Sîkrî, 125
Hauz, or cistern, of Jahângîr, 51
Hawâ Mahall, Fatehpur Sîkrî, 122
Hessing, John, 38, 103
Hîmu, Hindu general, 20
Hiran Minâr, Fatehpur Sîkrî, 125
Hospital, Fatehpur Sîkrî, 117
Humâyûn, 11, 12, 83; life of, 16; tomb at Delhi, 17

IBÂDAT Khana, 23, 115 *n.*
Ibrâhîm Lôdi, 4, 11
Itmâd-ud-daulah, 27, 86; history of, 86; marble tracery in tomb of, 88

JAHÂNÂRÂ, 32, 58
Jahângîr, life of, 25; connection with Agra, 28; cistern, or *hauz*, of, 51
Jahângîrî Mahall, Agra, 63
Jamaat Khâna, 83
Jâm'i Masjid, at Agra, 68
" " Delhi, 30
" " Fatehpur Sîkrî, 126
Jâts, 38, 43, 133
Jodh Bai, 67, 120, 121 *n.*

KÂLI, or Kalan Masjid, Agra, 102
Kanauj, 74; battle of, 17, 18
Kanch Mahall, 100
Kandahâri Bagh, Agra, 97
Karwân-serai, Fatehpur Sîkrî, 125
Kashmîrî Bazar, Agra, 29
Khâs Mahall, Agra, 59
Khurram, Prince, 28
Koh-i-nûr, 13
Kôkân, 5

LADLI Begam, 96

MACHCHÎ Bhawân, 53
Mîna Bazar, inner, Agra, 51
" " outer, " 46
Motamid Khan, mosque of, 29
Mubarak, Sheikh, 96, 132
Mumtâz Mahall, 29, 37, 71 *et seq.*
Murad, Prince, 30
Môtî Masjid, Agra, 30, 43
Muttra, 135

NÂDIR Shah, 38
Nizamudîn, tomb of, 32

Nûr Mahall, or Nûr Jahân, 26, 27, 28, 37, 57, 85, 94
Nûrmahall Sarai, 16

PAHALWARI, tomb of, 102
Palace at Agra, 30
,, Delhi, 30
Panch Mahall, Fatehpur Sîkrî, 118
Pânîpat, battles of, 4, 11, 20
Peacock throne, 38, 75
Pietra dura, 75, 89
Pigeon's House, Fatehpur Sîkrî, 125

RÂM Bagh, 15, 93
Reinhardt, Walter, 38, 103
Roe, Sir Thomas, 16, 26
Rushanârâ, Princess, 33, 35, 36

SALÎM, Prince, 25, 68
Salîmgarh, 67
Salîm Shah, or Sultan Islam, 17, 40, 68
Samarkand, 5, 6, 74
Samman Burj, Agra, 27, 57
Sanjin Burj, Fatehpur Sîkrî, 125
Shahdara, 28
Shah Jahân, hand and seal of, 15; life of, 29; monuments of reign at Agra, 33; death and funeral, 58
Shêr Afsân, 25
Shêr Shah, 17, 18; tomb at Sasseram, 18
Shîsh Mahall, Agra Fort, 62
Shuja, Prince, 30
Sikandar Lôdi, 4, 97
Sikandra, burial place of Abkar, 4, 25, 26, 96; road to, 15
"Somnath" Gates, Agra, 62
Stone-Cutters' Mosque, Fatehpur Sîkrî, 130
Sûraj-Bhan-ka Bagh, 101

TAJ Mahall, 15, 29, 71; building of the, 72; designers of the, 74 *and Appendix*; intention of the, 76; description of the, 79; marble screen in the, 74, 81; tombs in the, 81, 82; Jamaat Khâna, 83; view from the river, 84; museum, 84 *n.*
Tamerlane, or Tîmûr, 4
Tavernier, 31, 74 *n.*
Terry, Edward, 16

UNDERGROUND chambers, Agra Fort, 60

VERONEO, Geronimo, 74 *and Appendix I.*

WAZÎR Khan's mosque, Lahore, 88

YOGI's Seat, Fatehpur Sîkrî, 116

ZÂMÂNI, Mariam, 4, 107, 118, 120, 131; tomb of, 101
Zohra, or Zuhara Bagh, 14, 94

THE END